Build Your BUSINESS

BB WEBB'S
"NOTES FROM THE HIGHWIRE!"

MW01629825

July 2017
To Heather —
Here's to your
greatest success!
Warmly,
BB Webb

Build Your Business
By BB Webb
ISBN: 978-1-62452-039-6
Insight Publishing
Cover Design: Steve Wilson
Formatting and Layout: Chris Ott

License Notes:
All rights reserved. No part of this book may be reproduced in any form or by any means without prior written permission from the publisher except for brief quotations embodied in a critical essay, article or review. These articles and/or reviews must state the correct title and contributing authors of this book by name.

WHAT PEOPLE ARE SAYING

BB has the unique ability to turn vision into reality and obstacles into opportunity. While most of us only dream of success, BB succeeds in her dreams. We all need the kind of courage BB has to take that next step. Truly one of the most dynamic women I have ever known; we can all learn a lot from BB. Thank you for your friendship and advice.

—Fred Rich, CEO, Olympus Worldwide
Chauffeured Services Transportation

BB Webb is an entrepreneurial force of nature who knows what it takes to make things happen. No matter what season your business is in, this practical and engaging book will equip and encourage you.

—Ken Coleman, Author of
*One Question: Life Changing Answers
From Today's Leading Voices*

If I were to characterize BB Webb, I'd say she was a colorful hot air balloon able to float and fly upside down. That's what she does, takes the impossible, makes it possible, and then helps everyone else learn how as well. Read her book. Spend time with her. You'll be glad you did!

—Laura Whitmore, Private Investor

Be encouraged to continue beyond Ms. Webb's first few business basic chapters as she moves swiftly into real-life business challenges with a heartfelt and raw honesty. A captivating read, her stories expose the grief, astonishment, savvy, and brawn that move her into hard won successes. A gifted storyteller, BB demonstrates how becoming an entrepreneur can turn your life "right side up," providing both personal growth and life lessons beyond your wildest business dreams and imagination!

—April Wood Reeve, CEO Vivify Publications

In her new book, Build Your Business: BB Webb's "Notes from the High Wire!", BB shares her experience so that we can each learn, hopefully with less risk and less pain. This book is a must read for all the business owners and leaders I coach and every business and executive coach I train. Thank You BB, for sharing your experience with us all."

—Lee Huffman
Author, Speaker, Business Coach and CEO
Professional Development USA, LLC

BB Webb is a passionate writer and powerful storyteller. Not only does she share her own tales of hope and disappointment, survival and success as an entrepreneur with her readers; she does so in a language that's gripping and colorful, entertaining and witty, no-nonsense and often, disarmingly funny—just like the real-life BB Webb.
—Katja Ridderbusch, International Journalist

BB Webb's new book gives insightful, real-world business experience advice and speaks truth in lessons learned. Whether you are about to take flight with starting your own business, have been running a business for years, or just want a gosh darn good read, BB's sage advice mixed with a touch of humor is sure to add to one's personal and professional growth.
—Marilee Davis, President
Davis & Associates Public Relations/Marketing

"In her book, Build Your Business: BB Webb's "Notes From The Highwire!", BB tells it like it is. She's conversational, no-nonsense, and straightforward. Anyone who's started a new business will find themselves nodding in agreement. Those just starting off in business will appreciate the honest heads up. BB, where were you when I was starting my business?"
—David Krash, CEO Cotton Cravings
Organic Confections

PREFACE

It's safe to say, if anything's "safe to say," that we initially start our businesses because we have a passion. You've found what I call, your "twirl," what makes you feel ecstatic, alive, you feel as though you're living on "purpose," have found your passion.

Soon the realities of business are upon you. You started out, let's say, with a passion for creating, baking and designing awesome cakes. Soon you realize you need to market your services, handle complex operations, hire and train employees and most of all, keep the revenue coming in while remaining compliant with HR policies and how payroll taxes should be administered. You find you are spending less and less time doing what you actually love, which is designing and baking awesome cakes!

My book is a series of chapters dedicated to sharing what I've learned with over 11 years in the business of owning my special event venue, Carl House, and hosting primarily, extraordinary weddings and special events. My "Notes from the Highwire" are hard lessons learned in often how *not* to do business. I share as well epiphanies on how to develop best practices, whether your focus is online sales, or a "bricks-and-mortar" business, managing a team, providing a fine service or stellar product, or rolling out a new profit center. Business basics prevail for all business genres.

I know for sure that without passion, tenacity, and the ability to pick yourself up following mishap after mishap, you *won't* survive. To those who *can* and who *are* willing to learn from their "mis-decisions" and challenges that *will* occur as a business owner, my hat's off to you. There is no college or graduate program that will teach you what you'll learn from being in the "trenches"! My wish is to have a small part in helping you find, or re-find, your "twirl"—your passion—in a sea of unbelievers, naysayers, and governmental restrictions.

Regardless of the task at hand, my mother shared throughout the years, again and again and again, "Honey, you can do it!"

As I prepare myself for the next great idea to be developed in my ever-growing "bucket list" of business ideas, I still believe that life *can* be as abundant as we choose and our own form of "rainbow"! Here's to "possibility thinking," moving forward "as if" you will be successful and going for that pot of gold!

With compassion for, and warm wishes to your imminent success!

BB Webb, August 2014

DEDICATION

Having traveled through my share of "ups and downs," I know that being a business owner, innovator, and entrepreneur is not for everyone. I dedicate this book to my fearless and loving mother Kitty Vogel and my determined, ever-providing father, Bob Banta, both entrepreneurial spirits.

My father followed in his father's footsteps in a small tile, marble, granite business in Pennsylvania, which he passed along to my brothers Jeffrey and Johnny Banta, both of whom successfully grew the business.

My mother was a constant innovator of small businesses while playing her role as wife and mother during an era when women in business were much less encouraged or prominent. Her creative inventing inspires me to this day, as does her infectious, joyful spirit!

Though no longer living, I am grateful for the influences they both had on me. A photo of each hangs above my coffee pot where I'm sure to see them every morning, giving me a wink and encouraging nod!

TABLE OF CONTENTS

CHAPTER ONE
Putting Legs on Your Vision: Moving Forward "As If"

Keep your dreams alive. Understand to achieve anything requires faith and belief in yourself, vision, hard work, determination, and dedication. Remember all things are possible for those who believe.
—Gail Devers (1966–) Retired three-time Olympic Champion in Track and Field for the US Olympic Team

At last. You've thought about it, talked about it, dabbled in it, and now you're taking your "great idea" to the next level—you're going to start a business doing what you love! You've talked to friends and family, maybe visited the SBA (Small Business Association), to find out how to get started. You are in the bona fide "honeymoon" stage and it's "all systems go"! You're about to become a business owner. It may be an idea you've dreamed of for years. For me, it was the convergence of circumstances that pointed me in a clear direction, as well as a very clear voice in the back of my head! Luckily, I was listening!

I remember the exact moment when the idea came to me to create my event venue business, Carl House. I was standing in a room of an old mansion I'd come to co-own with my husband at the time. I was managing a challenging rental situation and was standing in what is now the "Frassand Room," named after a beloved grandmother. I was frustrated with the renters who were not paying on time, who were painting over one-hundred-year-old wood, clearly prohibited within our contract.

I had recently moved to the small town of Carl, an hour outside of Atlanta, to be a wife and stepmother (all firsts), having previously worked in the arts as a transient, creative spirit all my life. I knew I needed a project—something to create that could be good for my new family, good for the community, and profitable.

The Voice of Intuition

I was standing in the back corner of the room, consumed with frustration with my current renters, wanting more in my new "life situation," craving a creative project I could "own" and develop. I next heard a very distinct voice say: "This would make a great place for people to gather and have parties."

I know listening has been a skill I've worked to develop, though not always with great success. My mind moves at gunshot speed yet, I clearly heard this voice! I looked around the room and in the hallway to see if anyone else was in the house. There was no one.

It was instead that "voice" that guides us if we're quiet enough to hear—to hear our voice of intuition. Coming through shockingly clear, it told me there might be a better solution for this old and lovely home.

My inspiration to create a "gathering place" was quickly endorsed by my husband at the time. He is a man with multiple skill-sets; chief among them the talent to envision an old house resurrected. He would later remodel this home with old wood, tin ceilings, marble and granite (a must for me), and fabric on the walls. I would be the driver of the business, the person inspired to develop the, "nuts and bolts" activities within the business, how it would run day to day, hiring, managing, etc., while he guided the reconstruction of this historic and beloved mansion, circa 1903.

If this was to be the place where people would "gather and have parties," I needed to learn what kinds of parties might prove profitable. Reconstructing this old home was going to be pricey! I would quickly be in charge of servicing loans, upcoming payroll, and company bills through monies procured by this still undeveloped company.

I determined fairly quickly that creating a restaurant would be too risky, not guaranteeing the business traffic I would need. I would require more revenue to satisfy the growing vision and construction plans for the house. Upon investigation, I learned that the wedding industry was a sustainable and growing market. I researched what was needed to accommodate the needs of brides, their guests, and others desiring a special event venue, and what services might be most profitable.

I liked the idea that I could forecast ahead an evening of two hundred guests eating chicken *beurre blanc* with orzo pasta seasoned with fresh herbs, pecorino cheese, and steamed, seasonable vegetables. I liked knowing that I could see my future business on the books, promising needed revenue. As I worked the numbers, I quickly found that I would need it sooner rather than later!

Gaining Clarity of Vision

As I visited other venues throughout the southeast, I learned that this beloved mansion would need more work than anticipated. It would need to be gutted and restructured to add modern conveniences including air conditioning, additional bathrooms, and a commercial kitchen. In visiting similar historic homes with many small rooms, I knew we needed a large room to accommodate a higher number of guests, allowing them to all be together in one room. This would prove as a keen differentiator to other historic homes I researched.

Soon a ballroom with tall windows and a classic, curved staircase was envisioned and with it, the price tag all this "creating" was demanding. A large outbuilding was necessary to accommodate freezers, walk-in coolers, and storage space. An extension onto the current kitchen was planned to allow stoves, ovens, refrigeration, ice machines, and ample prep areas.

As the vision for my company grew, so did the financial requirements for creating this space. With a proposal to the bank, projected monies needed, and a timeline for getting the money with construction about to begin, I knew I needed to get busy selling to satisfy my upcoming loan requirements.

Little did I know what it would take and how arduous the days ahead would soon become for us. Fortunately, this was pre-2008 and loans were easier to procure with a sound plan and collateral back up should there be a disaster.

There were certainly glitches to our plan and some major lessons learned. Chief among them was that we would have benefited from a strict budget and better consideration of all the costs involved. As I began outfitting the venue with furniture, gathering all the items and staff needed to open Carl House, I was over budget by $89,000, a sum outside my secured loan. My only option at the time was putting this debt on various credit cards, which is *not* something I'd advise, though my only alternative at the time.

As an entrepreneur, you need to determine your level of risk tolerance. I took tremendous risks in not outlining all startup costs accurately.

With loan and credit card payments upcoming, I began booking events at the venue long before construction was completed. I created a vision statement and had designed a representative website, complete with photos of prospective brides and images of what the venue would look like when finished.

Grand Opening: Vision Becomes Reality

Fast forward less than a year from my "Joan of Arc" voices, despite a variety of rather hefty setbacks (a promised loan stalled, slowing construction, torrential rains that spring, and a marriage that was slowly dissolving), I opened July 5, 2003, with my builder putting the last nail in a wall as the bride and her wedding party entered the home.

The bride and groom left some specialty champagne that I remember we enjoyed while sitting back in the lavishly appointed groom's room, fondly admiring what we'd created. This was our first moment amid the scurry of planning, building, and doing all that needed to be done, to sit and wonder at the miracle of it all.

My significant takeaway from that stressful spring was adapting the attitude of moving forward "as if"—as if we would open on time and be successful doing so. Changing a bride's wedding date is tantamount to blasphemy, it's just not done. I realized I had no room for doubt in getting things accomplished to provide for my first bride's wedding. Putting blinders on to achieve my set goal was an important lesson.

It was at this moment I realized the value of what I later coined "solutions thinking." I've been enthralled to learn since then, my own capability of creating good and better solutions. Just as being a savvy sales professional takes a great number of "no's" before you get the inevitable "yes," I've come to learn what was stated beautifully in the film *Best Exotic Marigold Hotel*:

> *Everything will be all right in the end and if it's not all right yet, trust me, it's not the end.*
>
> —The Best Exotic Marigold Hotel

Tenacity and perseverance always win and if you haven't got that fiery spirit, being a small business owner might not be your cup of java!

I often ask myself, would I have done it any other way? Knowledge is a curious thing and you don't know what you don't know, until you know it!

Developing Business Savvy and Courage

I started my adult career as an artist, for I yearned to create. My enthusiasm and passion was for creating the next show, developing a character, exploring a new idea. It was not work; it was passion.

> *In the realm of ideas, everything depends on enthusiasm . . . in the real world, all rests on perseverance.*
>
> —Johann Wolfgang von Goethe

It's our job as business owners to become business smart. The best way to do this is by surrounding yourself with the right people. Similarly, I put a high value on recognizing inspiration and passion and leading from each. Businesses would not get off the ground if we stopped to figure out every detail before moving forward.

As parents, consider how much you knew about child rearing before actually having a baby. My guess would be, very little! Yet, you forged into parenthood with maybe a guidebook or two, but mostly, you learned along the way!

> *Magic is believing in yourself; if you can do that, you can make anything happen.*
>
> — Johann Wolfgang von Goethe

A measure of both enthusiasm and passion, along with planning and resoluteness, is necessary in building a successful business. My own passion, hard work, and fierce tenacity saw me through the struggles and lack of experience in starting a business, along with the support of the people who helped me get going.

A measure of naiveté helps us start endeavors we might never begin if we knew all the obstacles we would encounter!

Create a plan, do your research as best as you know how, engage others who have been there for support and/or advice, and then "go for it," and don't look back. The mistakes are mere stepping-stones for the growth you desire and you'll be promised one heck of a ride!

CHAPTER 2
Ships Ahoy! Vision, Mission and Values Within Your Organization

We've all heard the story of the cobbler whose kids didn't wear shoes and the businessman who was so busy with work assuring others had shoes, he failed to tend to the needs of his family. A similar irony or misstep is the organization president who either has a vision whose managers and employees alike don't follow or, equally bad, a company with no vision at all.

Early in my business career, I learned that not everyone thought the way I did. Arrogant or naïve, I was shocked to learn how much I had to explain about service, attention to detail, quality, and my expectations for excellence within my company. As a former business coach shared with me:

> *Communication is the response you get.*
> —Lee Huffman, CEO Professional Development USA, LLC

I realized that if I was neither clearly communicating what I wanted within my organization, nor getting expected results, I was to blame. Follow-through is as important as communicating a message that can be heard and understood.

As is for the captain of the ship, our responsibility is assuring that all our shipmates know where we're going. That means we need to have, in writing, what our company is all about, and the more simply explained, the better. I learned that creating a grandiose vision statement for my company, replete with descriptive adjectives and many lines of copy, no one really "got" what we were about at Carl House. When asked by others to recite my vision, even I, the creator and former actress, used to memorizing scripts, could not remember my own complicated vision statement!

After much creative back-and-forth with my team years later, we developed something short and memorable. At my special event venue we create, "extraordinary, memorable events." We later made that our marketing by-line as well.

> **As the captain of the ship, our responsibility is assuring that all our shipmates know where we're going.**

There is great discourse on the definition of both vision and mission statements. To me, a vision statement is the umbrella that surrounds all you do as a company. Everyone who works with you, employees, vendors, and customers should know what your company is about through your clear, concise vision statement. Similar to a mantra for living, a vision statement guides all that happens within your company. Your mission statement can state *how* you execute your vision. Ours is simply:

Carl House Vision: To create extraordinary, memorable events!

Carl House Mission: At Carl House, we are committed to making our clients' event dreams happen through careful and compassionate listening, honest communication, and expert guidance and service from our loving team. We unite in our commitment to offering total excellence and gracious attention to every person who comes through our doors.

Other vision/mission statements I find inspiring in their clarity and brevity include:

- Coca Cola: "To refresh the world, to inspire moments of optimism and happiness, to create value and make a difference."
- Skype: "To be the fabric of real-time communication on the web."
- Google: "To organize the world's information and make it universally accessible and useful."

I've read many vision statements that in their verbosity dilute the true intent and the clarity of what the organization is about, falling prey to unspecific and confusing jargon.

I came across a blog titled, "*Mission Statements: The Good, The Bad, The Terribly Misguided,*" by Cara Ellison, stating what she felt were some of the most non-descript, ineffectual vision/mission statements. I agree.

To maintain Playboy enterprise with many windows of opportunity to expand the Playboy franchise and develop other related entertainment franchise globally by leveraging Playboy's strengths of publishing, brand management, and marketing.
—From the unofficial mission statement from the Lady Hefner's *Playboy*

My question, aside from Playboy's desire to grow and expand as a business, what is it they do? I think we all have a *much* clearer idea of what Playboy is about that has *nothing* to do with the statement above!

Consider the precepts of clear, memorable, and concise when writing a vision or mission statement for your company. It should be something that others— especially your team—can easily remember and recite. What sets you apart from your competition and can both speak to and inspire your employees, customers, and the owners alike?

What makes your company what you want it to be? (You don't have to be there yet.) It might be the intention of what made you go into business in the first place! Make it short, grammatically correct, and free of nonsensical or industry-specific, confusing language.

Some favorite short, succinct non-profit organization vision statements include the following:

- Feeding America: A hunger-free America (4 words).
- Human Rights Campaign: Equality for everyone (3 words).
- National Multiple Sclerosis Society: A World Free of MS (5 words).
- Habitat for Humanity: A world where everyone has a decent place to live. (10 words).

I might change Habitat for Humanity's name to be more simply, "A Home for Everyone"!

A vision is the guiding light in your organization and the mission statement—how you move toward that goal. The culture or value statements within your organization are the parameters within which you live to accomplish your goals.

Building a Culture that Unites Your Organization

My organization has twelve culture statements, some of which I adapted from other organizations and others I created with my team or on my own. Periodically as a team, we review our culture statements in their entirety, to see where we might tweak one statement or another. We also consider if we are following our self-proclaimed code of conduct or if something needs to be changed.

Carl House's Dozen Points of Culture or Values:

1. **Commitment:** I am 100 percent committed to the vision, mission, culture, and success of Carl House, its current and future team, and its clients at all times. What I promise is what I deliver. I always make agreements with myself and with others and I am willing and I intend to keep these agreements.

2. **Ownership:** I am truly responsible for my actions and outcomes and I own everything that takes place in my work and my life. I am accountable for my results and I know that for things to change, first I must change.

3. **Trust, Heart, and Integrity:** I respond to whatever life brings with an open heart, and trust, that whatever happens in my life—positive or negative— is an opportunity for my personal growth and learning. I always speak my truth.

I communicate potential broken agreements at the first opportunity and I clear up all broken agreements immediately.

4. **Personal Excellence:** "Good enough" isn't good enough at Carl House. I always deliver products and services of exceptional quality that add value to all involved for the long-term. I look for ways to do more with less and stay on a path of constant and never-ending improvement and innovation. I totally focus my thoughts, energy, and attention on the successful outcome of whatever I am doing. I am willing to win and allow others to win. I display my inner pride, prosperity, competence, and personal confidence. I am a successful person!

5. **Communication:** I speak positively of my fellow team members, my clients, and Carl House in both public and private. I speak with good purpose using empowering and positive conversation. I never use or listen to sarcasm or gossip. I compassionately acknowledge what is being said as true for the speaker at that moment and I take responsibility for responses to my communication. I greet and farewell people using their name and with a smile. I always apologize for any upsets first and then look for a solution. I only ever discuss concerns with the person or people involved or my manager.

6. **Diversity, Willingness, and Gentleness:** I am committed to improving my life and the lives of my clients and teammates alike. I strive to celebrate and value differences and similarities in all people. Learning from each other in a supportive, caring environment is a powerful way to grow into the best people we can be. The power of my own willingness to learn from others and my ability to show gentleness toward myself and toward others help us all grow together in a loving, kind, and sacred way. I know I can make a difference and that I am valuable just as I am, as is everyone I come in contact with in my world. I send positive thoughts to everyone with whom I have contact.

7. **Education and Continual Learning:** I am committed to my own growth and to continual learning. I learn from my mistakes and forgive myself when I am in error. I consistently learn, grow, and master so that I can help my fellow team members and clients learn, grow, and master also. I am a student and an educator and allow my clients and teammates to make their own intelligent decisions as I make mine. I impart practical and useable knowledge rather than just theory.

8. **Teamwork and Team Mentality:** I am a team player and team leader. I do whatever it takes to achieve team goals at Carl House. I focus on cooperation and always come to a resolution, not a compromise. I am flexible in my work and I am able to change if what I'm doing is not working. I ask for help when I need it and I am compassionate to others who ask me and I make time to assist them if I can.

9. **Balanced Living:** I have a balanced approach to life, remembering that my spiritual, social, physical, educational and family time is important as is my financial and intellectual time. I complete my work and my most important tasks first, so I can have quality time to renew myself and to spend time with friends and family or to give back to my community.

10. **Joy, Fun, and Gratitude:** I view my life as a journey to be enjoyed and appreciated. I create an atmosphere of fun and happiness so all around me enjoy it as well. I am a truly grateful person. I say thank you and show appreciation often and in many ways so that all people around me know how much I appreciate everything and everyone I have in my life. I celebrate my wins and the wins of my clients and team. I consistently catch myself and other people doing things right!

11. **Systems:** I always look to the system—clear processes and procedures—for a solution. If a challenge arises, I use a system correction before I look for a people correction. I use a system solution in my innovation rather than a people solution. I follow the system exactly until a new system is introduced. I suggest system improvements at my first opportunity.

12. **Abundance:** I am an abundant person! I deserve my abundance and I am easily able to both give and receive. I allow abundance in all areas of my life by respecting my own self-worth and that of all others. I am rewarded to the level that I create abundance for others and I accept that abundance only shows up in my life to the level at which I allow it. I freely give to others, as I know that celebrating my own abundance only brings me more to enjoy and share.

Short or more descriptive as the ones we developed at Carl House, culture/value statements should provide the framework and structures to which all action and behaviors align within your organization.

When a team member or owner acts outside of these guidelines, the conversation might first begin with the way your organization handles, for instance, communication. Instead of making your team members "wrong" for perhaps speaking unkindly behind another teammate's back, the conversation might be around the culture you are working to create as outlined in your culture statement guidelines.

Just as a family holds dear certain values, bringing on employees from a variety of cultures, backgrounds, and family experiences, will have an effect because they all have different ideas about excellence, work habits, and communication styles. Creating a culture within your organization of one hundred, fifty, or two employees is paramount to maintain consistency with how issues, work in general, and communication with customers, vendors, or within the team is handled.

In my next chapter we will explore the idea that: "The way you do anything, is the way you do everything."

The way you do anything, is the way you do everything.

If you're careless and inconsiderate at home, chances are you're careless and inconsiderate within the work place. Vision, mission, and culture statements help to guide behaviors to ensure everyone is moving in the same direction on the ship that you, as owner, navigate within your business. Use these guidelines as your "ships ahoy!"—your call to action on how you want your business to run!

CHAPTER 3
How You Do Anything Is How You Do Everything: Building Your Brand

Though I tend to gravitate toward a sense of personal style, I am often approached by a friend or colleague I've not recently seen with a comment such as, "You've changed your hair style!" or "Your hair is a different color!"

"Well, yes," I reply. "Why wouldn't it be?"

Their slightly quizzical look tells me of their surprise!

It is our right and delight as human creatures to invent, create, and to change. I relish my freedom to invent, create, and to change!

I've had team members come to me saying, "Last week you said you wanted it this way."

"I know I did," I respond, "I've changed my mind; I think this way now is better."

Change is good and necessary, though with a team, it must be communicated clearly. I perform well with a high level of risk and I relish a measure of constant innovation and change. Not everyone is comfortable in such a life space.

There are many good companies that can supply worthy personality, behavioral, and preference profiles. These profiles can be helpful for team members to both appreciate and better understand why a teammate may work differently than he or she does, become upset in certain situations, or be impassioned and enthusiastic in others.

We need all types of people, work styles, and skill-sets to successfully run a company. I'd jump off a building if I came into a cubicle each day, doing the same thing, in the same way. Add to that working with numbers and spreadsheets and I'd ask for an immediate lobotomy!

What one person finds motivating and what they "live for" might totally bore, frighten, or set another person's hair on fire.

DISC is one profile that I have found helpful in learning my own proclivities and preferences, and those of my team. My profile points toward leadership, a need for freedom, and a desire to inspire, create, and persuade. I'm great in front of a crowd, good at building rapport and rallying others around an idea.

Similarly, these same "good qualities" we have, can turn negative if not in the right balance. My ability to guide, lead, and inspire when taken too far, can become pushy, abrasive, careless, or manipulative.

Clarifying Your Brand

A brand is your mark as a person and for your business. I have a certain way I dress, manner of speaking, personality, temperament, and style. It's part of who I am and part of what I've developed for myself. It's authentic for me.

Far more than a logo, creating a company brand and style is imperative so that others know who you are, what they can depend on, and preferences they need to adopt if they work in your company. Brand consistency must permeate your entire organization. Its consistency needs to be with the way your team speaks, the way they dress, how phone calls are handled, issues managed, deportment, and your evolving systems, practices, and protocols. Way more than just your business cards and Web appeal, a brand extends into all aspects of who you are as a business.

Consistency does not preclude change. I've changed many things within my organization throughout the years, though not my consistent intent for excellence, comprehensive services, attention to details, quality, service, and so on.

> *Of course I'm inconsistent! Only logicians and cretins are consistent!*
> —Tom Robbins, Even Cowgirls Get the Blues

I share a story in one of my talks about one of a plethora of "pet peeves" I have. I have no qualms admitting that I am heavy with preferences and points of view. As a business owner, you are paid to be preferential. If you aren't, your company brand will suffer.

I love to grocery shop. I have a busy lifestyle though, and relish when I can make the time to stroll down the aisle of my neighborhood supermarket, considering recipes I'll make, and imagine an evening of entertaining guests at home—a clear passion.

At the end of my grocery experience, I come with my wealth of carefully selected goods to the checkout counter. I am always recruiting good talent in my area and at the counter I find a young woman slouched, leaning hard on her left hip, chewing gum. With hair unkempt, her green nail polish chipped, she wears no make-up. Our conversation, initiated by me, goes something like this:

BB: "Hi, how are you today?"

Checkout Person: "Oh, I can't wait to get off today," she says as she smacks her gum.

I can feel myself becoming unglued!

BB: "Really, why's that?"

Checkout Person: "I've been working since 9:00 AM, I'm tired."

(Note: It's 2:00 PM). I feel the parent/business owner in me about to pounce.

BB: "You sure are lucky to have a job."

Checkout Person: "*This* job? Ugh. I hope I win the lottery."

BB: "What would you do if you did?"

Checkout Person: "I wouldn't work here! I'd sit around all day and do nothing. If I wanted, maybe buy a cool car."

With that I'm rushed out as the next person moves in on me. Having just spent $203.45, I feel I deserve time to get my things together, gather my receipt, and maybe receive a "thank you!"

BB: "Will you give me just a moment to put my credit card back in my wallet?"

Checkout Person: "Oh, yeah, sorry."

There are so many things wrong with the above discourse I hardly know where to begin! Most of all, I am upset that a reputable grocery chain would lack better coaching or not be aware of what the front line people are saying, doing, and how they compromise the organization's brand.

Several things hit my radar immediately:

- There is no dress code or guidelines on appearance, as she looks like she's barely stepped out of bed.
- She's made no attempt at putting herself together. Her nails look bad, roots are showing in her hair (and this is not Carrie Bradshaw from *Sex in the City* making a fashion statement), and she's chewing gum!
- She speaks badly of her company.
- She's not engaging me, the customer, about my experience and what she can do for me.
- She clearly does not feel valued by her company, neither does she value the company or her job.
- She is fairly quick at getting me rung up and out (probably why she was hired), too much so, and I feel rushed and unvalued.
- Her grammar is slack and she doesn't say thank you as I leave.

Wrong, wrong, wrong! Though I would hope this young person might be more aware, it's the responsibility of management to train the team. She is on the front line of interaction with customers and she's lost my vote, entirely. Sadly, this is a grocery chain near my house; it's convenient and one I enjoy, except at check out time.

On the other hand, the women in the grocery's bakery (in particular the manager, Diana) are fabulously helpful, friendly, and complimentary. I feel valued when I order a cake. I'm asked about my preferences, how I am feeling that day, if I need anything else, or if they can carry something to the car for me.

There is utter inconsistency within this store and it weakens their brand and certainly my experience.

If you don't pay attention to the important details of your business, your customers will, and then move on to your competitor.

> **If you don't pay attention to the important details of your business, your customers will, and then move on to your competitor.**

Creating a Meaningful Brand

Some areas to consider when establishing the brand within your company:

Do you have a consistency of style within all your marketing collateral, colors, fonts, and overall look and feel? If so, how would you describe it? Does it tie back to the vision, mission, and culture statements within your company?

At Carl House we work with a variety of wedding professionals who partner with us in creating the event our clients most envision. I'm careful to partner with professionals who reflect our similar attention to detail, care for the client, and overall excellence, regardless their product or service.

In working to bring on a new partner to assist us with linen services at our events, I met a lovely young woman who owns a wonderful linen company. Her company was going through a logo rebranding. With great enthusiasm she shared with my marketing director and me her new logo.

In looking at the image, we both froze in silence. I'm clear with all the professionals who work with my company that feedback is imperative to us. I want to know when we could do something better, differently and, of course, when we've done well. Most of all, I want to develop relationships with people where respectful communication and feedback work to help us each grow and improve.

This person's last name is Harbour and her company provides gorgeous linens for all kinds of events. Their products and services are top notch. She calls her company, Harbourhouse Linens. It's lovely if you want to utilize your name in your company name, though I'll urge, only if that choice makes sense. Her logo was an image that was intended to look like a lighthouse tilted on rocks in a harbor.

Our silence grew. I was measuring how to give my feedback to be both respectful and supportive, as I have great respect for both her and her company. The shape, size, and tilt of this "lighthouse" resembled, to me, a very well endowed and extremely happy male appendage. I respectfully told her so, mentioning that I did not have a propensity for finding "naughty" images in logos, but this one was rather glaringly obvious. In asking others within my company about the image, their agreement was unanimous.

She responded that she and the designers didn't feel that it looked like an x-rated image, but a lighthouse in a harbor. I shared that "they" are not your audience, but "we" are.

I respectfully and honestly responded, "You might ask around a bit to hear what others see in it. I want you to be successful, and if people are distracted by the image in your logo and what it represents to them, you might consider an alternative."

Be open to other opinions. It's easy to become attached and to hold your branding "precious," but don't. If it doesn't say what you intend it to say, it won't help your business grow. Don't use your name in a logo unless it makes sense. I'm still unclear how a lighthouse relates to linen services.

Is there a consistency of dress, style, and personal appearance within your team? What is your dress-code; do you wear uniforms?

We work with a wonderful bakery at my venue with the clever name of "Sugar Kneads." The owner has a delightful, funky style with pink highlighted hair and tattooed cupcakes on her wrists. She carries the same style and "pink" to the artwork on her truck and with the clothes she and her team wear. It's fun and perfect for her business. She's developed a style that works for her and within her company.

At my venue I require a polished style for my team. We outline "polished" as assuring that your hair is neatly arranged, if you wear make-up, that it is tastefully applied and appropriate business attire.

If I ran a skateboarding company, our brand and style would be different. We'd all wear brightly colored, sporty "skorts" and trendy nail polish colors. We'd greet people at the door on a skateboard, have our hair pulled back in pony tails, and say "Yo" a lot!

I do not own a skateboard company. I own an elegant special event venue where we cater to brides, encouraging them to trust us for what will no doubt be, thus far, the most important day of their lives. In addition, their event might be one where they possibly spend more money than at any other event in their lives.

I'm preferential about the language my team uses. We don't refer to what a bride has to invest as her "budget." I find the word holds a restrictive, limited feel. I prefer instead that my team ask about the "spending range" they'd prefer to stay within, or preferred "investment," as it is our duty to be aware of this parameter.

Similarly, I refer to the colleagues we work with within the industry not as, "vendors," despite that being the vernacular in the industry, but as "wedding professionals." That's what they are—professionals!

I'm from Pennsylvania, a Yankee at birth, where calling everyone, "you guys," is as commonplace as sweet tea is in the South. Still, I ask my team to refer to our clients and to one another as "y'all," "all of you," or, "ladies," as we are south of the Mason-Dixon Line and working within an antebellum style mansion, with brides, who are not "guys" at all!

Additionally, I have recently required that my team not respond to a request from me, a client, or guest with, "no problem," but a more positive response. "No problem" holds the negative connotation of a "problem." I wonder: "Why would it be a problem? I've hired you for the job!"

Might the response not be phrased instead (as Chick-fil-A and Ritz Carlton have established in their organizations), "your pleasure" or "I'd be delighted to help." Those responses hold an energy and a feel that I greatly prefer!

How are challenges handled within your company, with the client, and within your team? Do managers have a consistency in style with regard to mentoring and disciplinary actions?

> How are challenges handled within your company, with the client, and within your team? Do managers have a consistency in style with regard to mentoring and disciplinary actions?

It's very important that a style for handling issues that arise in your company is consistent and dependable. I'll address systems, procedures, and protocols in a later chapter.

Brand Starts with Vision and Extends into Marketing

Do your website, ads, newsletters, and what you say and do on social media all work together in a consistent way that represents who you are as a company? When people talk about your company, what do they say?

Each impression made by your company—a phone call, one-on-one with a team member, to a client, what people see online and in ads and marketing collateral—must hold a consistent look and feel. Ask and listen to what people say about your company.

If communication is indeed the response you get, what *are* people seeing from what you communicate through your marketing, through your team, and the processes and protocols they follow? How do the words, actions, dress, and systems within your company and collateral materials reflect what you want people to see in your company?

If what you hear from clients and colleagues is not what you want, it's time to determine where the holes are in your intended brand image. Make the way you do *anything* be the way you and your team do *everything* to move in the direction of your vision, mission, and your company's values and culture statements.

With this consistency of intent, adopting new and better ideas as your company evolves, watch your company and the satisfaction of your team, and the delight for your clients grow. I'll bet you a dollar that your revenue will grow as well. And isn't that what it's all about—pleasing your client, nurturing the talent within your company, and watching your profits increase?

CHAPTER 4

The People You Hire, the People You Fire: Hiring the Right Team for You

Do not hire a man [or woman], who does your work for money, but him [or her], who does it for the love of it.

—Henry David Thoreau, Writer, Philosopher

One employee can make or break a company. Similarly, an owner, along with his or her vision or lack of vision and the execution of that vision, can make or break a company!

I once gave a talk titled, *The Seven Lively Spins for Developing Your Business,* as opposed to, *The Seven Deadly Sins for Destroying Your Business,* all of which I've committed times twelve.

Utilizing Your Many Talents

Having begun my career as an artist, I had no real experience in a business environment. Yet, having written, produced, and toured in my own one-woman play across the country, I did have some talent for marketing myself.

I remember finishing my itinerate tour in Hammond, Louisiana, where I stayed with a lovely family. I was hired to teach a few workshops, perform my show, and be the guest artist in a play my colleague had written.

I remember arriving in town without an ounce of energy. I was beyond exhausted. I'd been traveling throughout the country in my little red pickup truck, performing and marketing my play, conducting workshops, doing tech for my show, rewriting the next show for the upcoming season, or driving myself to my next "gig."

Though it was empowering to learn my capabilities—to create, sell, market, and produce—doing it all was exhausting and too much for one person. I found that in having to wear so many "hats," I had little time to do what I most enjoyed, which was writing and performing. Cash flow was a constant issue and I soon learned that traveling alone without friends, moving from place to place without community, was not a choice I wanted for the long-term.

> I also found that in having to wear so many "hats," I had little time to do what I most enjoyed, which was writing and performing.

In graduate school, the options for an artist/performer were to go to New York City or Los Angeles, neither of which I relished. I wanted to create a one-woman play and take it on tour. My business plan beyond that was limited.

Sheer tenacity and will took me through a few years of artist residencies and unglamorous touring throughout the United States. Upon landing in Atlanta in 1993, with exhaustion plastered on my face, I knew I had to do something different.

Like quitting a job, I moved my focus elsewhere, with the more onerous challenge of letting my image and years spent developing as an artist fall to the wayside. Little did I know that the part-time server work I took on with a variety of catering companies in Atlanta during that time or how working in sales with a management consultant firm, would serve me when I began my own special event venue. Certainly my experience of creating, developing, producing, and selling my work as an artist was a valuable skill-set with my upcoming business.

The Art of Hiring Well

Mindfully hiring and developing talent is one of the most important responsibilities of a business owner. Endeavoring to be a "one person show" is a definite liability. I have hired and fired scores of people to work within my organization. Throughout the years I've significantly improved my hiring criteria and processes. I've learned to better know when it's time to release someone to other, better fitting opportunities, yet find I am still challenged to know who will ultimately be the best fit.

> Mindfully hiring and developing talent is one of the most important responsibilities of a business owner.

Hiring talent is a bit like dating—you can share your resume (or online profile), get references, but not until you are "in bed" together, sharing the work, demonstrating how you handle the job, adversity, and feedback, you just don't know what you don't know. Certainly personality profiles help, but like a marriage, you just don't know if it's a fit until you know it's a fit. Time vets out all people!

With shifts in the economy and some more traditionally transient roles within my organization, there are times when my business has seemed like a bus station with people coming and going in rapid succession. There have been many times I've kept people long after training and coaching have failed and, similarly, there are no doubt actions I might have taken to keep dedicated, trainable individuals when I didn't.

What I know for sure is that when you have the wrong person living within the walls of your organization, their influence works like a cancer, eating away at the careful fabric you have worked to design, challenging growth, morale, and your vision for the organization.

The right people can take your organization to places beyond your vision. Though money is a necessity for us all and certainly a motivating factor for some, assuring that your employees are working in areas where they feel impassioned, valued, and supported is of key importance.

Knowing your own strengths and weaknesses around bringing others on and whether you are the best person to manage your team or only a select few is key. I do best working at a high level, sharing my vision, developing new ideas.

Though I've often worked in the "trenches" and know the importance of coaching my workforce, managing the details is neither my strength nor my place of passion. It is my job instead to find qualified people who can manage my vision effectively. Had I the wherewithal or vision while working in the arts to gather support for the areas where I was less adept or less impassioned and, had I figured a way to finance such support, I might have continued on.

Hindsight is like an elusive lover, with the greater emphasis on what you have right in front of you. Had I not experienced all I had as an artist, or certainly the challenges within my own business, I'd not be where I am today. I've found adversity to be my best friend and coach!

Developing Healthy Skepticism
Here are some things to consider when hiring:

A clear plan and process for hiring is key, as is a framework for training and evaluating a new-hire's progress. I have in the past so badly desired a new-hire for a needed position and been so eager to bring help on board that I overlooked warning signs of the person being an ill fit. I met a woman years ago who introduced me to a term I use often: "healthy skepticism." Healthy skepticism suggests that you move slowly, remain optimistic, but take your time in assessing the person or situation.

Apple creator Steve Jobs was in favor of a collective hiring process with which I concur. People who will be working with a new-hire need to weigh in and assess capabilities. They need to have the opportunity to ask questions and to voice concerns. It is they who will be training and working with the new person. They need to have the opportunity to give a perspective separate from the person who does the actual hiring.

A colleague of mine introduced me to a new way of interviewing candidates. I find it helpful in more ways than one. The process begins as follows:

1. You cast as wide a net as possible for placing your ad—job boards, newspaper, industry newsletters, LinkedIn.
2. The interested person is instructed to call a number for step one of the interview process.
3. A dedicated phone line is used (not your main company line), and when interviewees call, they are welcomed to your company's "applicant line" and asked to answer three questions. These questions will tell you several things:
   a. If the applicants can follow directions.
   b. Give you a sense of how they sound, their energy, and ability to communicate.
   c. Depending on the question, how clear and concise they might be when asked to come up with an answer to a common issue within the role they are applying.

The more savvy applicants realize they can listen to the three questions, hang up, and prepare answers to give when they call back. I had one applicant so flustered by the process that she pulled herself out of the call-back ranking by getting tongue-tied, then saying:

"Oh s--t, I knew I wouldn't get the job anyway."

She was right!

You are able to screen the candidates who seem most qualified through this process.

4. The next step is inviting respondents who seem most qualified to meet you and your team. These are the applicants who seem the most able to follow instructions, answer questions, and deliver. This is typically done with a phone call during which they are asked to bring along a resume and three work references. They are asked to dress in the manner befitting your company (e.g., business professional, business casual). Let them know how much time will be needed. Ask your applicants to bring questions they might have about your company, the position, and anything that will help them know you and your team. What they ask will additionally help you know them.

You can learn a lot from watching people before the actual discussions begin. Clearly a new process for many people, there is often a level of discomfort until we share with them what happens next.

At the group interview, I suggest bringing in key members of your team.

If I am involved in the interview, I will typically introduce the group to my organization and team and thank everyone for his or her time. I explain next that they'll have the opportunity to share about themselves and to answer questions that we have of them. I share that I feel the best hiring fit must be mutual to be successful—we must be a mutual "right fit" for one another.

My team then introduces themselves, sharing how long they have been with the company, what their position is, why they love what they do, and some of the challenges they've faced. They also share some of their future goals within their position and in the company.

I've found this process puts applicants at ease. Soon most are comfortable sharing about themselves and they possibly feel encouraged to ask more questions after hearing some of the responses and questions of the other applicants. I had one person tell me at the end of one of our group interviews:

"I was nervous at first, but it felt like a very supportive group chat by the end of the time together. I learned a lot about interviewing, watching others, and about the company and its values."

At break time anyone not interested in the position, based on our sharing, is encouraged to leave. I had one candidate share with me during the break that she was not comfortable with so much "touchy-feely," or working in a gay friendly environment. I was happy that she was wise enough to disqualify herself.

Everyone is then thanked and resumes and references are collected. The applicants are told that we will review their resumes and that we will invite the candidates we are interested in interviewing further for a one-on-one interview. We shared that we would let all applicants know of our decision.

Usually only two or three people stand out from the group interview, saving time and money. This process gives your team a chance to be a part of the interviewing process. Having influence on who is being hired is empowering to a team, especially because they will be working with the new person being brought onboard.

The next step is a meeting with your team on their perceptions and then getting references, references, and more references for the candidates who stand out favorably. I recommend getting a background check on each candidate as well. Be sure that the person who does the reference checking knows the proper questions to ask and what legally is off limits.

In a phone reference-checking conversation, I like to learn something about the prospective employee's style of working and a sense of how they fit in with a team they've worked with in the past. They could be the greatest worker, boasting a grand set of credentials, but if a person is difficult to work with, it might not be the fit you most desire. Consider "healthy skepticism" when first meeting someone. Allow the person the time to demonstrate to you how good he or she is.

You Now Have a New-Hire. What's Next?

Hiring someone new is only a small piece of the "hiring" puzzle. It took me years to develop an orientation process. For each department, manuals and job descriptions are all a continual work in progress.

I have learned to use ninety-day goal sheets where employees outline four to five major focus goals for a three-month period. Also called key performance indicators (KPIs), they help to measure new-hires' successes within the job in an area designated to discern how their goals support my goals as business owner. I've found this to be a great coaching tool to document work accomplished, for giving feedback, and determining priorities and accountability.

I've also utilized something I call "action reports" as opposed to "issue reports." Their purpose is to coach and document key areas of concern in performance with a plan for corrective action as necessary. Letting someone go without proper warning, coaching, or documentation is both unfair to the employee who wants to do well, and it also puts a company at risk for paying out unemployment where it may not be warranted.

It is also expensive to replace someone when a good corrective action process can both correct the action and save the team member in the process. If you do go all the way through the process, you have enough documentation in place to show that your team member was terminated for good cause.

However small your company is, it's necessary to do some sort of formal review of what the employee is doing well and where he or she can improve. I'm much more comfortable issuing praise than criticism. An employee won't grow or have the ability to know where he or she might work to improve performance without helpful feedback.

As a business owner, I am responsible for doing so, or delegating this task, coaching, reviews, and how I want things done to my management team.

Keep Your Friends Your Friends

I learned early on that my employees cannot be my friends. Far from meaning to sound harsh in this regard, our role as business owners is different from that of our employees and these differences should be respected. As difficult as it may be in a small company to discern the difference between these roles, certainly when you work closely with your team, the need to do so is paramount.

Your rights as owner are different from those of employees. It is in your best interest to value the input of your team and to be sure their work experience is positive, that they are trained properly, and have ongoing opportunities for growth and support. Keep in mind that they do not take on the same risks you do and should live by different guidelines than you do. I endeavor to lead by example, though I also have benefits and risks that my employees don't share.

Be friendly, for sure, but caution against taking into confidence an employee who might have information that works against your goals for your company when he or she leaves or is asked to leave.

I like George Bradt's summary of bringing on new talent:

> The only three true job interview questions are: 1) Can you do the job? 2) Will you love the job? 3) Can we tolerate working with you? That's it. Those three . . . every question, however it is phrased, is just a variation on one of these topics: Strengths, Motivation, and Fit.
> —George Bradt, U.S. management guru and blogger *Forbes* (April 27, 2011)

CHAPTER 5
Priorities Are Where You Invest Your Time: How to Tell the Difference

The key is not to prioritize what's on your schedule, but to schedule your priorities.
—Stephen Covey, Educator, Author, Businessman, and Speaker

I learned that we can do anything, but we can't do everything . . . at least not at the same time. So think of your priorities not in terms of what activities you do, but when you do them. Timing is everything.
—Dan Millman, Author and Lecturer

Language can be perplexing, the meaning of words are diluted with usage. I felt compelled to look up the definition of the word *priority* to assure that you and I, as reader and author, were on the same page, so to speak. Below is a definition for priority that I found on www.dictionary.com.

Noun, plural pri·or·i·ties for 2–4.
1.   the state or quality of being earlier in time, occurrence, etc.
2.   the right to precede others in order, rank, privilege, etc.; precedence.
3.   the right to take precedence in obtaining certain supplies, services, facilities, etc., especially during a shortage.
4.   something given special attention.

Adjective:
1.   highest or higher in importance, rank, privilege, etc.: a priority task.

My takeaway then is that a priority is something that takes precedence—is of greater importance than something else. One activity takes precedence before another in your focus and attention.

As a business owner I find I need to discern weekly, daily, and sometimes hourly which activity or seeming "fire" to tend to. I think that many things seem to be a priority. In my younger years as an artist, I learned to juggle balls and clubs for a children's show I performed. Discerning priorities to me is a similar feat, and it's easy to drop the "ball" if your priorities and decision-making skills are off.

Discerning Your Priorities

As business owners, our focus should be on two main areas: growing profitability within our companies and assuring our primary asset—our people—are well managed and trained to run key aspects of our organizations. This can be a curious balancing act involving another key factor: self-management with the time I have available. Both my time and that of my employees must be prioritized wisely.

I worked years ago with a terrific counselor who shared that "priorities are what we spend our time on." I prefer to think of it as time invested rather than spent.

I like to think my time is invested, rather than spent.

What is the difference between investing and spending? With an investment I expect a return and make adjustments to maximize that return. With spending, I consider that whatever is spent is gone, depleted. I prefer to fill my time with investments, be that time invested with friends or in my business; with each I am hoping to either give or receive a return.

With regard to any given priority, we may say that working out three times a week is a priority in our lives, but when our child is sick, or our business fumbling to bring in necessary cash flow, priorities change. Time allocated for play, or to other things of importance, new projects, and so on gets temporarily put aside as we can't do all things at the same time. We need to keep the things that we say are important at the forefront.

I experienced a time in my business where the fatigue from moving past challenges in the economy hit me hard. I was spending time with poorly selected employees or I experienced my own improper management of them. Our audits of business practices that we thought were in proper order, but weren't, mounted. I was in survival mode, working to serve our current clients, managing ongoing challenges and threats, and keeping the company above water in a quickly shifting economy.

It's Just Weather

I call these traverses in business terrain "weather." Wait awhile and they shift. *That* you can count on. The "thunderstorms" in business provide water for the garden that is your business, and if you're paying attention, the most arduous times create the greatest lessons for growth. The pendulum swings and we are again soon enjoying the other things on our very important priority list.

"Maslow's Hierarchy of Needs," is a theory developed by Abraham Maslow in his 1943 paper, "A Theory of Human Motivation." In it he stated that people are motivated to manage certain needs. When one need is fulfilled we seek to fulfill the next one, and so on. In order for us to make one choice, we must forego or delay others. If we choose to take on one opportunity, we decline another, if we choose one partner, we decide against any number of others.

Despite the pervasive, "have-it-all" mentality prevalent certainly in Western culture, all things cannot be done at once; we must choose. Perhaps in time, with a long life and the blessing of surplus stamina, energy, and drive, we can choose various priorities during a given period of time. But all at once only certain things are possible.

When starting my Carl House business, I learned that to grow the business I needed help, which meant I needed start-up funds. With the loans I had taken on, there was no time to wait for revenue to come in, as loan repayment waits for no one.

I knew I had a love for visioning how my business would work, how the profit centers within it would expand, and how we would market our services and products. I knew I could get sales started and inspire a new team. But, I also learned quite quickly that I needed savvy and passionate sales professionals, as this was not my greatest point of passion or expertise at the time. I needed someone in love with working with brides, our main clientele, and someone who would be overjoyed detailing our clients' wedding preferences. I knew also that to succeed I'd require an adept finance person, as that was clearly not my area of expertise.

I started with a small team to help me grow and knew that as we started generating revenue and profit, I could add on to my team. This way, I would not burn out from overwork as I'd done producing, marketing, and performing my one-woman play. I knew it would be essential that I stay within my immediate skill-sets and passion points in order for us to succeed and grow the business.

The Value of Taking a Break

I was listening to a short "Ted Talk" by Arianna Huffington, chair, president, and editor-in-chief of the *Huffington Post* Media Group and nationally syndicated columnist and author. With perfect comedic pitch, she espoused the importance of a good night's sleep. I couldn't agree more. I smile a bemused smile when I hear businesspeople speaking about how hard they worked and how little sleep they got, as if these admissions are crowns of glory.

To me, a day or week filled with the things I enjoy most is something to brag about. Having slept eight hours gives me great joy and a thoroughly rested body, which is much more effective at work or at play. Managing our various responsibilities in a smart way and delegating appropriately is something I would instead brag about achieving, not how poorly I used my time depriving myself of needed rest or food.

All managers and most true business owners are, essentially "knowledge workers," a term popularized by management guru, Peter Drucker. The term "knowledge worker" typically characterizes workers who engage primarily in the acquisition, analysis, and manipulation of information as opposed to the production of goods and services. In the mid-1970s the University of Michigan released a study that knowledge workers could work sixty to seventy hours per week with good productivity for about four weeks. Then, with each additional week they worked that many hours, their productivity dropped off by 10 percent to 20 percent per week, until their actual productivity from their sixty to seventy hours was actually twenty-five to thirty-five hours.

These workers were present physically, but their minds were not. This can have a hugely negative impact on an entire organization. Get some rest, take a break, schedule time for fun! Do something that really gets you excited. You can then go back to a fifty-hour week and get a better return on your time investment.

Additionally, consider taking quarterly breaks to stave off the tactical demands of your business long enough to form well-thought-out strategies for moving your company forward.

> Additionally, consider taking quarterly breaks to stave off the tactical demands of your business long enough to form well-thought-out strategies for moving your company forward.

We can count on shifts in the economy and changes in what customers desire and are willing to spend on. To be savvy business owners, we have to weather current changes and have a willingness to change what isn't working or alter what might have been a priority at one time to something else. Agility is key, along with the ability to look ahead like a captain at sea, anticipating the next storm, change in tide, or whale wanting to capsize your ship!

> To be savvy business owners, we have to weather the current changes in tide and have a willingness to change what isn't working or alter what might have been a priority at one time to something else.

Determining Levels of Urgency Within Your Organization

Working in a small business with a clear vision in place, my team and I often wear a variety of hats and have more work on our plates than can easily be done, certainly in the time I'd prefer. Utilizing ninety-day goal plans and weekly task lists with accountability measures helps my team organize their variety of duties. I assist in managing what tasks need to be accomplished first, second, and third.

As business owners, we tend to think that everyone thinks in a similar style to the way we do with regard to urgency or order of importance. Just as communication is the response you get, it is key to clearly express and have in writing what is of prime importance in any various role.

Years ago when reviewing our sales, I asked my finance person at the time why we hadn't received the monies for six weddings that had taken place. I had a policy of getting all monies up front and before we ordered food or alcohol for any event. The woman seated in the finance role said to me: *"I'm supposed to collect the money? I thought the wedding director did that!"*

After picking myself up off the floor, I explained clearly that yes, she was supposed to collect the money. Soon after that I included in her job description and in the manual that a key priority was to assure all monies were collected from clients before each event! Thankfully all money was eventually collected, minus $1,000 from one person who never returned our call—a small price for a significant learning curve.

Creating a Structure for Prioritizing

So, if priorities are where your team invests their time, it's key that time is spent deciding what these priorities are. Put a process in place to assess the changing priorities in any given day, week, month, or year. While you're doing that, factor in good food and plenty of sleep and time with folks who nurture and uplift you.

I was engaged as a speaker at a conference recently. I got to know one of the presenters who shared with me something interesting. In day-to-day life we all have a variety of issues we contend with, certainly true as a business owner. He had recently overcome a severe cancer diagnosis and was fortunately in remission. He shared with me that when you are healthy you have a variety of issues, problems, challenges—call them what you will—but when you are sick, you have *one problem* and that is your priority—to heal.

Take care of yourself with sleep, good food, and exercise, even if at times you can fit in only a moderate amount. These should be toward the top of your priority list because without health, you have nothing. It's foremost on Maslow's hierarchy of needs, and on my own as well. I promise that choice will serve you well, and the lives of the people you love the very most!

CHAPTER 6

Selling What You Do: Creating and Communicating Value

Your value doesn't decrease based on someone's inability to see your worth.

—Ritu Ghatourey, Indian Author

Any business sells. We sell our services. We sell our products. If oil is the life-blood of a car, then sales is the life-blood of your business. Every individual within your company should be aware of this fact and that sales are what create their jobs. Everyone in your business should be a sales advocate for your organization with some aspect of training on how to talk about what your company does and what you can provide to the right customer.

Surprisingly, workers within organizations forget this rather obvious fact (sales making their jobs possible), and often mindlessly work without understanding the nature of the engine that creates the positions that allow them to live, work, and grow.

As owner, it's your job to keep them aware of the need to be an advocate for the brand within which they work! You and your team need to be open to improving what happens in your business so everyone involved is proud of where they work, how work is done—the vision, mission and culture within the organization—and how prospects and customers are treated and your services or products provided.

There are scores of books written about how to sell, sales theory, sales structures, processes, guides, tips and preferences. To me, selling in the simplest of terms is about finding out what people need, assessing whether you have the solution to satisfy their need, and communicating the value you offer. It is through genuine caring, building of rapport, and matching a service or product with a need that the sales process begins and from which sales professionals can succeed.

We've all been "sold to" and then not heard from our seller after the sale. I chuckle when a sales call comes into my business asking for the owner, Mr. Carl. If they'd do their homework, I might respond. My business's name is Carl House, I am Ms. Webb. We can all share dozens of less than genuine or attractive sales situations.

Redefining "Sales"

I encourage you to remember the times when you've purchased something and remember it fondly. It might be that you don't remember because it didn't feel like a "sale." It felt instead like someone was sincerely tending to your needs and being concerned about what was important to you. You felt heard, helped, and guided. You may have ended up purchasing something at a greater cost than you initially set out to invest because this person helped you better understand what you really wanted, not what you were perhaps settling for instead! You later realized what your sales advisor said was true—you would not regret allocating a little more money to get what you really wanted or desired.

I recently purchased a foreclosed flat in Atlanta for an in-town office and was planning to put granite on the countertops. Trained since my days in the arts to be frugal, I picked out what seemed a lovely piece at the lower price point. When the installer called, I shared that I was from a marble and granite family in Pennsylvania, my grandfather being the patriarch of the business, followed by my father and now brothers who moved to Montana and started a stone business there. I expressed that I wanted to make them proud when they came to visit, enjoying the granite I was planning to install to upgrade my flat.

The installer, a sure-spoken young woman named Amy, shot back, *"This granite won't make them proud!"*

I was stunned by her sharp retort.

"Oh, why?" I asked, momentarily despondent.

"You may want to come in and see the different slabs of granite," she answered. "The one you chose is really quite dull and nothing special. It's hard to tell from looking at a small sample piece. The next grade up has many more stunning options."

I considered the extra $500 it might cost to get something more pleasing. I visited the store to see the actual slabs, and Amy was right. Though I hadn't intended on paying the additional money, I'm happy I did. The granite I chose instead of my first selection was far and above worth the extra expense. Good job Amy, you heard my request (to make my family proud—and me), and you spoke up!

There are other ways to provide value to your clients and to assist your prospects to help them make a decision to buy from you. Within my Carl House business, our primary service/product is weddings. We provide a gorgeous venue, the culinary products and services to manage the event, wedding direction, in-house floral design, and full set-up and take-down services. We're pretty much a one-stop-shop for the bride and her family with the ability to refer great wedding professional partners to accommodate all their needs.

> There are other ways to provide value to your clients and to assist your prospects to help them make a decision to buy from you.

In addition, we provide extras such as linens, rental items, a photo booth, or various trendy "culinary action stations" to allow for a variety of choices to help customize the bride's event according to her vision. We recently added a product/service that I envisioned and developed with my team called Wedding Dreamz™, to assist brides and grooms in financing the wedding of their "dreamz" through donations by friends and family.

Managing Expectations While Communicating Value

Brides come to us after having watched many wedding planning reality shows, movies, and having explored all manner of Pinterest sites and blogs featuring outstanding and expensive weddings. Yet, with a plethora of new venues opening in my area that charge less than our average wedding with our high level of service, attention to detail, and premier facility, brides want the same pricing these neighboring venues offer. Far from an "apples to apples" comparison, our job is to help our brides see *all* that is included with our fee and how a Mercedes is different from a Toyota. They're both nice, but different. Even so, similar to a Walmart mentality, we are told again and again that "Venue B is offering the same menu package at a percentage less than our price."

While it may be true that venue B can offer the same menu package at a lesser price point, the quality of the food, quantity of food, timeliness, service, and so on is not comparable. However, if what our bride says is true and the competition is a similar brand to ours, it is our job then to demonstrate a greater value for choosing us, or to adjust our pricing to encourage our bride to choose us. Adapt, persuade, or die!

In training a new salesperson on my team, I asked about a particular prospect. Mother and daughter had visited our venue two times and shared their limited spending plan. (Again, I ask my team not to use the word "budget," as it holds a restrictive connotation; I prefer the more intentional, "spending plan" or, "investment").

They had limited dollars to create a wedding that would equal anything we might produce on a popular Saturday night. We have created lesser minimums on days other than our most popular Saturday evenings. Fortunately, this bride was open to a Sunday morning where we have more venue fee flexibility. Regardless, they were concerned about affording the other services needed within the total amount they felt willing to invest for her very important ceremony and wedding reception celebration.

Before meeting with these prospective clients, I asked my salesperson what feature within Carl House, or within her overall wedding, was most important. To this bride, it was making a memorable entrance in the dress she had picked out a year before. My venue features a gorgeous, curved staircase, perfect for any grand introduction. This was a key piece of information, as I know very few other venues share this unique feature. I was sure to emphasize this differentiator and to help her envision her grand and memorable entrance down our classic curved staircase.

I next asked what their total spending plan was, including offerings we did not directly provide, such as photography, DJ, and cake services.

Upon giving me the total amount they were willing to invest, I immediately considered my network of wedding professionals, colleagues who could help and who would greatly value my referral. Since this family was Hispanic, I asked if many of their guests were Spanish speaking. I saw the bride's mother light up:

"Yes, many are!" she said.

With equal enthusiasm I shot back, "I work with a terrific DJ who is bilingual, has worked with me for more than ten years, and who I'll bet will work with you on pricing because the wedding is on a Sunday morning. Do you mind if I give him a call?"

Upon her agreement, I immediately picked up the phone and was delighted to speak to this colleague of mine, introducing him to my prospective clients. He warmly introduced himself and shared that yes, he was available on the date they chose and would be willing to work with them on pricing. I also shared with them that his wife is a terrifically talented photographer and that they might consider bringing her onboard after looking at her work.

I hung up the phone with multiple wins. I created a solution for my prospective clients that would save them money with alternative needed services. I assisted in their planning by setting up a meeting with not one, but two colleagues who could create affordable and high quality solutions for them. The added feature of a bilingual service provider was a real plus. I didn't need to lower our pricing or the value of what we were providing and after the call I asked for the sale:

"So, I am envisioning you coming down our beautiful staircase as man and wife! Have you decided to become a Carl House bride?"

Tears and hugs and an affirmative, "Yes, *yes*!"

Additionally, I passed on good work to two colleagues who will in turn refer us in good favor. I secured a threefold win without cutting our prices!

Creating Mutual Wins

Sales is about being creative, working your network, negotiating and genuinely looking out for the welfare of your prospect. If everyone wins, you win, always. I always ask,

"What can I do for you?"

When we speak about branding at my company we speak about both our company branding and personal branding. We all buy from people we respect and trust, or given the choice over two people, always the person we can relate to, whom we feel has our best interests in mind.

The best salespeople I have encountered are easy to be around, they aren't trying to "sell" me, push their business cards in my hand, or blather on about what they do. They instead take a genuine interest in me! Colleagues who have helped me the most are ones I want to extend a hand to, referring them for solutions that my company, other colleagues or friends need.

Creative Ways to "Touch In"

When connecting colleagues, or offering a business solution to someone, I suggest not merely an email saying:

"Lawrence, meet Josie, Josie, meet Lawrence," with words of praise for each person and contact information, but a follow up telephone call.

"Lawrence, BB Webb here. I'm checking in. Were you able to contact Josie and was the introduction helpful?"

I use SendOutCards.com to let both people know I am thinking of them and hope the connection was helpful.

SendOutCards are computer-generated, hard copy cards that are both cost effective and personal. You can customize your own cards or choose from over 17,000 greeting card selections for one of your many touches when contacting a prospect or thanking a colleague. They are easy for my team to use and efficient. Hand written cards are great too, though I find with the ease of using SendOutCards, we send out over 50 percent more cards than we did with handwriting. They take less time, are inexpensive and their choice of fonts is much better than my, "chicken scratch" hand writing!

The sender merely picks a desired card and font from the company's website, or personally creates a custom designed card, adds the name of the person they choose to contact, along with their address. The SendOutCards company does the rest. In our Constant Contact, Mail Chimp age of email marketing (which I endorse as well), who doesn't like receiving a personalized, hand-written greeting card? I know I do! And I generally sit it on my desk; the sender's exposure continues!

Sales is a numbers game and you need strategies for filling your pipeline. Not everyone will liken to you or your brand. As Jeffrey Gittomer so aptly puts it:

"Obstacles can't stop you. Problems can't stop you. Most of all, other people can't stop you. Only you can stop you."

And, something I learned from taking constant rejection as an actress:

> *Success is the ability to go from failure to failure without losing your enthusiasm.*
> —Winston Churchill

Create a vision, develop the plan, be consistent, be creative, keep learning, surround yourself with encouraging people, and don't give up! This along with pure tenacity has won me more rounds than I can count!

CHAPTER 7
Friends Versus Friendly: Nurturing the Relationships Around You

It's hard to tell who has your back, from who has it long enough just to stab you in it . . .
  —Nicole Richie, American Fashion Designer, Author,
  Actress, and Television Personality

Everyone suffers at least one bad betrayal in their lifetime. It's what unites us. The trick is not to let it destroy your trust in others when that happens. Don't let them take that from you.
  —Sherrilyn Kenyon, Best-selling American writer

You're the boss. Some people won't like you. There will be a honeymoon stage, there always is, but know that a hot shower of remorse will visit you if you expect the people you hire to adore, adulate, praise, agree with you, thank you for your sacrifices, understand why rules are different for you, celebrate when you take a vacation, or expect that you "hung the moon."

Similar to the role of a parent, these are not expectations you should have. Find another purpose! Release the need to be understood and loved by everyone; it's not in the cards, neither should it be. Taking on the responsibility of growing a business is a vastly different role than working for someone. Period.

Find a dog to dote on you and follow you around with a smile; employees won't and shouldn't. If somehow you are able to inspire, encourage, and coach with a positive result, great! Get your ego out of the way.

In my early years in business, I met with my attorney to update my will. I added in three employees who helped me grow my company the first few years. These were years I didn't pay myself, but brought them on board and together we worked to create events and as much structure as we could, while working many hours to get the business going. They were, especially by today's post-economic crash era standards, and the size of my business, well paid. I intended to bequeath them a part of my company. I named my mezzanine after one woman. This was year three. I was both naïve and unseasoned.

Later that year I took three of my start-up ladies to Italy for a week. It was glorious. A friend of mine owns a gorgeous villa where we stayed and I paid for airfare, passports, meals, and incidentals on the trip. Some had never traveled abroad. I loved being the provider, creating new experiences. I was the boss, but I felt that I was their beneficent friend as well. I enjoyed doing this, though in retrospect, I should have been building a cash reserve to protect jobs within my company.

Fast forward to 2008 and the economic crunch. I had begun to take time away from my company to develop other things. I'm the owner; this is my right and privilege and had always been my plan. I traveled on a three-week, "personal growth sojourn," my longest getaway to date. I entrusted the health and running of my company to my team.

I returned with cash flow as low as ever. We had scant reserves, sales at the end of the month were at $20,000; I needed $120,000. A $42,000 septic system issue nearly closed us down during our busiest time of the year. My partner in a large land deal defaulted and the bank from which I had secured a $1 million-plus loan was releasing all loans in the hospitality industry, and in Georgia. I had taken my eye off the ball and had nearly lost it all.

Upon approaching my three directors to help create solutions, I was asked if they together could meet privately with a favored business coach I periodically worked with at the time. They wanted to discuss issues privately with him, as they weren't comfortable discussing them with me.

I felt terribly betrayed.

"Why can't they speak individually with me?" I thought.

I was the odd person out, now filled with animosity and doubt. I felt the division in our roles strongly. Any idea of trusted friendships with these women had sunk to a new reality. In working to get past our crisis, I found their solutions to be minor remedies. I had real decisions to make to keep my company running.

Like tearing off a bandage slowly, one by one I let all three people go, unable to support former salaries and feeling a breach in what I thought had been trust, open communication, and an honoring of each of our roles. I knew no other recourse to resolve cash flow and the feeling that I'd never get some of the relationships back to anything workable, given both the changes I needed to make and the lack of transparency I felt.

Careless Facebook rants made me out to be a, "narcissistic bitch" and photos of a parade of congregating former employees visited the pages of social media. I was pierced with hurt, feeling betrayed by some of the people I cared for deeply.

I was green, well-meaning, but sloppy and it all ended badly. When I finally had to let the last person of the trio go, I adopted a supervisory stance that was inconsistent with any former behavior and laughable. I had become my own worst enemy.

Keep Employees, Employees

I had made a grave and life-changing error, I allowed myself to become friends with my employees in a relationship that was not equal and over which I had wrongly crossed an important boundary. A business owner/employee relationship is not a democracy. A business owner takes all the risks and holds the power to hire or fire. Crossing that line can jeopardize your business, your reputation and, most of all, the promise you made to current and future clients, as well as the other people you employ.

It took me a very long time to recover from the hurt I felt from my lack of judgment and in trusting people I should never have allowed into my personal space or heart. In letting things become too personal, my company and I suffered. It is the single most difficult event I've experienced in my history as a business owner.

I asked another employee why the people I let go were saying such hateful things about me.

She cocked her head slowly to the side and shared, "You create a family-like atmosphere at Carl House and you kicked them out of the family."

I soon learned that one person with whom I had so openly confided, would soon be working for a competitor, airing my personal matters, sharing my vulnerabilities, and making light of struggles that created the very job she had once enjoyed.

A parent should not share intimate details about intimate conduct involving a partner to his children. Similarly, a boss should use discretion and consult a coach, counselor, or a best friend who understands business, regarding key issues with personnel or within his or her business or personal life.

Allowing Relationships to Teach You

There is no greater learning ground than one where you fall hard and recover. I am grateful for those experiences, the people involved, and all that I have come through. The same scenario has not and will not happen again. It was unfair to my employees and threatened the well-being of my company.

Build a network of real friends you trust, who have your back. Be friendly with your employees, create necessary structures, love them as a boss, be kind, be fair, be honest, but don't cross the line that jeopardizes bringing out the best in one another. Be the boss. Let them be your employee and appreciate their presence in your business, as you hope they'll appreciate the opportunity you made available to them!

Our actions are guaranteed to affect others. Because we are not alone in this world, much of our learning about ourselves comes from our interaction with others. Our relationships are our teachers. We learn from each other.
—Tae Yun Kim, Author, Seven Steps to Inner Power

How people treat you is their karma; how you react is yours.
—Wayne W. Dyer, Author and Motivational Speaker

CHAPTER 8

Encouraging Creativity Within Repeatable Systems: Processes, Procedures, and Protocol, Oh My!

How you climb a mountain is more important than reaching the top.
—Yvon Chouinard, Rock Climber, Environmentalist, Outdoor Industry Businessman, and Owner, Patagonia

True stability results when presumed order and presumed disorder are balanced. A truly stable system expects the unexpected, is prepared to be disrupted, waits to be transformed.
—Tom Robbins, American novelist, *Even Cowgirls Get the Blues*

As an artist and businesswoman, I relish tapping into each quadrant of my brain to help my business grow. I dearly cherish my ability to create and to be creative. I need it like a hummingbird craves sugar water. Call it left brain–right brain, I care not; I know I need space and freedom to create.

I read an interesting excerpt of, *Let My People Go Surfing: The Education of a Reluctant Businessman*, by Yvon Chouinard, who shares, "If you want to understand the entrepreneur, study the juvenile delinquent. The delinquent is saying with his actions: 'This sucks. I'm going to do my own thing.'"

I relate to a measure of that thought, though I would prefer to label myself, or other creative entrepreneurs, not as juvenile delinquents, but insistent dreamers with a cause and passion. Far from delinquent, the ability to show up again and again and *again* is necessary, despite the intermittent travail. I've learned that the use of thought-out, tested, repeatable systems makes the day-to-day of growing a business much more manageable!

Risk Taking and Creativity

One of my favorite artists, painter Henri Matisse, stated that *"creativity takes courage."* Both authors—Ray Bradbury and Kurt Vonnegut—have been cited as saying versions of the following quote with regard to risk taking and creativity: "We have to continually be jumping off cliffs and developing our wings on the way down."

This is true if you are a business owner. Not everyone has the same risk tolerance. There is much to know and understand about running "A commercial, profitable enterprise that can run without the owner"—Brad Sugars, Founder ActionCOACH.

Every business owner has a bit of warrior and action hero in him or her. A business needs a captain who holds a vision, along with creativity to both start the enterprise and to help guide it into itself. A business also needs structure.

My business needed more structure than I was adept at giving it when I first began.

Developing Systems, Processes, and Procedures

As I better realized the structures needed within my company, I found people better than I at putting together protocols and policies to consistently guide us in the direction we needed to go. With that, there are essential human resource policies that any business owner needs to be aware of to stay in accordance with the law.

> A business needs a captain who holds a vision, along with creativity, to both start the enterprise and to help guide it into itself.

Though you might not be large enough to have a designated HR person on staff, have a consultant nearby to check in with, as laws change quickly. You don't want to be caught not knowing something. When audits come, the government expects you to keep up with regulations. If you don't, there is no forgiveness for not knowing the law, only extra monies to dole out that can put your company at risk.

Similarly, everyone working within your company should have a job description and a manual as to how their jobs are done, what is expected, and how to perform each aspect of the job. It's one thing to envision how you want things to run, and another to create the step-by-step processes, along with necessary coaching of your team toward that vision.

Employees are not mind readers. I've been fortunate to share my vision of a role with key people I've hired. They skillfully structured the role I described, but most people need more guidance and direction to be successful. A leader's job is to set their workers up for success. To do so, I sometimes need to get out of the way, and at other times more guidance and training is needed.

Minimizing Your Liabilities

Stan Slap is the president of the international consulting company called, Slap. He is a creative and innovative business leader I admire. He is credited with revolutionizing performance for some of the world's biggest, smartest, and fastest companies, and developing strategies and buy-in from teams for implementing them. He shares: "Your company is its own competition and can deliver itself debilitating blows the competition only dreams of."

Inspecting What You Expect

I had an employee share a management supposition I like: "A manager needs to 'inspect' what she 'expects.'" I've been guilty of abdicating instead of delegating. The difference is that delegation implies follow-up and supportive feedback for the job performed. Conversely, when abdicating the job at hand is shared, perhaps with a vision, and is taken to mean, "good luck; I hope you do well," with no supportive touch-in to assist or follow up through the completion process.

I know many entrepreneurs who are not good managers of people, but excellent at envisioning and forging forward with their company vision often at a far greater speed than is advisable. They lack the structures needed that will easily guide their business forward in the desired directions, with systems that support growth, quality, and overall excellence.

Understanding Pace

I learned a very important lesson when training for the one marathon I ran, in New York City just after turning forty. I joke to friends that I was passed by an elderly nun (she actually wore her habit), and a fellow with one leg—all true. Both were much better runners than I! Though perhaps not my forté, I was delighted to have finished, despite our first fifteen miles of torrential, chilly rain. Toward the end of my training period, I read a book by running guru, Jeff Galloway. He coached that runners could advance their speed if they would run one mile and walk a minute.

I remember thinking, "I'm already fairly slow, why would I want to slow myself down further by walking twenty-six minutes in a 26.2-mile marathon?"

> His wisdom allowed that by walking, you rested just enough to give yourself greater momentum for moving forward and that it would actually increase your overall time.

His wisdom allowed that by walking, you rested just enough to give yourself greater momentum for moving forward, and that this would actually increase your overall time. I tried this and was surprised that he was right and it worked! (I am the truly stubborn entrepreneur who has to test a theory to actually believe its efficacy.)

As the, "keeper of the vision"—most business owners are—it is key to slow down the rudder of your ship from time to time to inspect the details of your business. By doing so, you are able to see how you might speed things up with better structures, processes, and desired protocols in place. The intention of this process is to work toward increasing profit margins and improving efficiencies and customer service to better grow your business.

In our sales and marketing department, we have processes that measure everything from the calls and e-mails received, to the number of follow-ups that turn into appointments and appointments that turn into sales. We look at zip codes to see where people are coming from and which marketing periodical or online wedding website they may have visited that leads them to us. Analyzing our Web stats helps us understand which marketing we should further invest in, and customer satisfaction surveys help us know where we did well and where we can improve.

Similarly, we have processes in place that further establish our branding. The way we greet a guest at the door, our dress, and the language and terminologies we use are all mindfully selected. We have a process in place for answering the phone, taking information, and how we send it to the person who was called to assure it doesn't end up lost on a sticky note.

I learned early on in my business, with a host of information in my head, that teaching someone how to do a job was great, having them execute your vision all the better. However, when they leave or are asked to leave—and they do or will—that information, if not written down, leaves with them. As arduous as step-by-step processes are to put in writing, not doing so creates a liability for your business and enormous work for you and the new people entering your company to recreate. Moreover, recreating the information is costly!

Encouraging the Creative Process and Personal Excellence

Everyone learns differently. I'm not the sort of personality who likes to learn a skill through reading a manual. I like to learn by doing, diving in. One of my most revered mentors was the brilliant Tony Montanaro, a philosopher, teacher, inspired storyteller, and mime artist. (Forget the cliché "white-face" mime, as this was not his focus, he masterfully used his body and mind to create mesmerizing and unforgettable realities out of thin air.) I've never met a man more gifted, deep in philosophical thought, spiritually alive and passionately Italian, playful, smart, and filled with heart as Tony.

Tony was the real deal and inspired me as a young twenty-year-old to create my own personal style of theatre. He inspired scores of young artists, dancers, musicians, mimes, clowns, jugglers, and assorted itinerant artists to develop their own personal style of theatrical expression. At weekly Friday night shows, we'd try out the new material we'd created during the week. Eager audiences would arrive in droves to the Celebration Theatre, in the far reaches of remote South Paris, Maine, to witness new work in the making.

The audience might watch a harpist who fashioned a harp securely around her waist to allow her to dance while playing Jimmy Hendrix, or a juggler-acrobat who hung upside down while balancing on a tower of seven chairs stacked on each other. I would test my character sketches—short monologues—I'd create of people I'd invented with a story to reveal. At these showcases we learned to bomb, crash, burn, and arise anew with great feedback from our audience and fellow artists on how to better create our pieces of new art. I learned the value of failure and realized, too, that "failure" was the wrong word.

Tony taught us to be curious about how to create the steps, actions, or words in each of our creations. With any character I created, I knew the message I wanted to share and soon the mannerisms or words spoken by the character would create the expression I envisioned. With curiosity, I would explore different ways to express the idea I had in my mind.

I appreciate Disney's philosophy on this creative trial-and-error mind-set:

> *Around here, however, we don't look backward for very long. We keep moving forward, opening up new doors and doing new things, because we're curious . . . and curiosity keeps leading us down new paths.*
> —Walt Disney

This same attitude is needed in creating processes and protocol within a company. Much like creating systems in a business where there is a need for a desired result, once created the process should be as easily repeatable as a stage performance.

I have brought Tony's talented wife, Karen, a brilliant and innovative dancer and storyteller, into my business to work with my team. She has worked with them to encourage creativity, to teach them how to fail and revise, and how to invest in their own personal excellence. She encourages this attitude whether to create better processes and procedures or in creating a mind-set of personal excellence in work done day to day.

Mix it up; bring in a diversity of people to coach your team. You might not have previously considered these people as having a beneficial and refreshing perspective.

Managing and Assessing New Ideas

I have no shortage of ideas. My true passion is developing the next new idea, profit center, product, or service. I've been guilty of not answering all the necessary questions to smartly move forward with a new venture. I have more than once begun something to realize the improbability of its working, given certain circumstances. I often learn soon that the logistics of making an idea work are not something I am willing to invest in, actually do, or delegate and pay others to do.

We have a phrase in my office if my team thinks I'm not listening to their concerns. If something I am moving headstrong into is causing grave concern, I've instructed my team to hold up a Defcon 1 sign. This warning is meant to mimic the "defense readiness condition" acronym for their alert system within the United States Armed Forces to signal a grave concern in the direction I'm headed.

Defcon 1 is the most severe of five states of alarm. This symbol is to alert me that if I don't look at what I'm doing more carefully, I might lose clients or money, actually both! In other words, I need to slow down and listen.

We have since developed protocols that include questions to ask for considering a new product or profit center. These questions help me look more carefully at the proposed profitability and the team needed to execute it. It helps me see how much I might need to be involved in the process once it's created and the overall cost. These are all key questions to ask to avoid needlessly focusing on things that won't move my company forward.

John Kao, trained in psychiatry and business, has taught creativity at the Harvard Business School for the past fourteen years. He has founded several companies in biotechnology, interactive multimedia, and feature films. He shares that: "The crucial variable in the process of turning knowledge into value is creativity."

Get your team together and map out a plan and process for each department. Do it as a group where you can see how together you can create structures that will help your company run with greater efficiency. Gaining this clarity will assist you and your team in creating greater profitability and value to your clients.

CHAPTER 9
Eye Spy: Knowing Your Competition

Never compete with someone who has nothing to lose.
—Baltasar Gracián, Spanish Jesuit and
Baroque Prose Writer and Philosopher

The early bird gets the worm, but the second mouse gets the cheese.
—Willie Nelson, Country Music Singer-Songwriter,
Poet, Actor, and Activist

Eye Spy: Knowing Your Competition

Competition is a good thing; it challenges us to be better. It's no mistake why Home Depot and Lowe's are often situated across the street from one another. I came across a great article titled, "Why Do Competing Stores Open Up Next to Each Other?" at http://weakonomics.com dated Friday, November 13, 2009. The author asserts: "The average consumer doesn't know what they want. They know they want to buy some tools, they know they need to get a prescription filled, they know they want to buy a car. They just don't know what to buy or where to buy it.

"Imagine that you're in the market for a car. You want a Honda Accord, Toyota Camry, Nissan Altima, or a Ford Fusion but you aren't sure what you want to buy. You want to buy a car today but the dealerships are spread across town and you only have time to drive to one location. At one individual dealership, your odds of finding the right car are one in four. This means your odds of not finding the right car are three in four. This means there is a 75 percent chance that no one will get a sale. Now imagine two of the dealerships were located together and you have time to visit both since they're so close. Now there is a 50 percent chance that someone will get a sale.

"Follow the logic and if all four dealerships are located together there is a 100 percent chance that someone will get a sale, meaning each dealership has a 25 percent chance of landing the sale when they are located together. If the Nissan (or any other) dealership were alone, then it would only have a 25 percent chance of being selected, and then a 25 percent chance of being the right car for the customer. These probabilities are multiplied and therefore each dealership, located separately, only has a 6.25 percent chance of landing a sale from you, the shopper with the time to only go to one part of town."

Clearly the above hypothesis is a bit simplified, but the fact remains: when competing companies are located together, their collective chances of successfully closing a sale are increased. Foot traffic is heightened and comparison shopping is made easy with the ability to easily investigate a number of similar products or services, while possibly getting a bite to eat nearby so you don't pass out from exhaustion with all your comparison shopping!

Shopping Your Competition

How thoroughly do you shop your competition to know that what you offer is competitive? Many of us have played "secret shopper" and donned a secret g-mail account or alternative cell phone and fictitious identity to find out things about our competition. I'm always curious as to how quickly someone from another venue might answer my call, how he or she speaks to me and their excitement about my pretend wedding. It's easy in my industry to get menus and price lists from other venues. That could be true in your industry as well.

I've found a "spying" concept I like much better than playing Maxwell Smart. I have invited venue owners to visit me at my venue. I've invited them for lunch or coffee to share details about my business and to ask what their key challenges are. As soon as they realize that I have nothing to hide, they tend to open up about challenges we both share. With an atmosphere of transparency and giving, I ask to learn more about how they do things and I show an interest in referring their venue, should we be booked, based on their venue being a similar right choice for a certain client.

My intent is well meaning and I'm certainly open to learning new and better ways to do what we do! My intent, too, is that our sharing might help both of us and that they too might be willing to refer us should they be booked.

This scenario is not unlike the Santa Claus in the movie, *Miracle on 34th Street,* who worked at Macy's. He referred Macy's customers to Gimbels when the Macy's store was unable to provide a desired product to an inquiring customer. If you are truly taking care of your potential customers, and you can't serve them, it's always best to give them not just a referral, but to pick up the phone and introduce them to your contact directly. They might not do business with you now, but they'll remember how you helped them and they will either refer you to others or come back to you another time!

It's a law of nature that if you help others, they are inclined to return the favor. We do this all the time at my venue and I find it a triple win. Our prospect is happy with an alternative solution, the other venue is elated to have a potential sale passed along, and I am happy because I have two raving fans who will no doubt refer my business to others. It's like gravity, taxes and aging, you can count on all three!

It's a law of nature that if you help others, they are inclined to return the favor.

It's important as well to stay current with what others are providing or selling at their business. With social media (particularly Pinterest) in my business, wedding blogs, and both hardcopy and online industry magazines, it's easy to stay current with new trends, colors, reception offerings, ceremony rituals, and design options. Your industry no doubt has similar resources online and in print, as well as associations you can join to help keep you current and learn about what others in your industry are doing.

Imitate and Adopt the Best

I've started many new profit centers within my business by paying attention to what other businesses were offering or what the reality wedding shows were providing. Soon after opening my business, I began offering the then popular chocolate fountain, later tapas style "action" food stations, cupcake bars where guests decorate their own, gourmet coffee stations, and recently, a trendy organic, multi-flavor cotton candy station that is wildly popular! I saw others doing it and I adopted their good ideas; why wouldn't I?

In our industry, there are many wedding professionals offering a variety of services that our brides need. I recall a gentleman who wanted me to offer his popular photo booth as an added value when booking with us. He of course would get the monies, leveraging (smartly I might add), on the monies we spend in marketing and advertising to his benefit. Smart man. He spoke of this growing popular trend, the ease of using the booth, and the relatively inexpensive cost to purchase one. He sharing that he had purchased ten booths which he brought to venues around my area.

He then noticed, as I tilted my head slightly to the left and looked puzzled. He stopped speaking and asked:

"Do you have a question?"

"*Yes,*" I slowly responded. "With all due respect, why wouldn't I just purchase a booth for myself and enjoy the profits you speak of, sir?"

He stammered a moment and then his eyes dimmed.

"I'm sorry," I said, "I'm happy to promote you and talk about what you do for other venue owners, but I'm always looking for new ways to bring revenue into my company. I think purchasing one would be a great fit for us."

Our photo booth has been not only a great offering and treat for our brides and her guests, but a worthy profit center, having paid for my investment in less than six months. In addition, each lovely photo strip includes the name of our bride and groom, the date they were married and our company name and website, not the name of the fellow who so kindly suggested that I sell his photo booth services to our brides.

I relish the idea of the hundreds of photo strip pinned to refrigerators across the southeast with our logo, name, and website printed at the bottom. What a win! I thank that kind gentleman every time I see him (and do share his name with other venues uninterested in purchasing an in-house photo booth)!

When people take your ideas and benefit from them, rejoice, as there is more than enough business for all of us. Having a photo booth helps to build awareness for other people offering the service. For example, if a guest attends a wedding at my venue and has big fun making photos in our booth, when she gets married at perhaps another venue, she'll remember the fun she had and look for a professional who offers the service, if the venue she chooses does not have one in-house. I've just helped drive business to the gentleman who was requesting I help sell his service. It all comes around.

It's key to stay on the cutting edge of what your clients want and helps you stay front and center in your industry. It is equally important to understand how your numbers need to work, while differentiating what makes you special and unique—your USP (unique selling proposition)!

Communicating Value, Being Nimble

What happens when pricing begins to change within your competition and you are challenged to continue to sell at your current price, or raise your price as your costs increase? In my industry, a plethora of new venues have opened in my area, with one underselling the next. I felt very challenged, despite the notion explored earlier—that these competitors were helping *me* close the sale. We had to be nimble and smart to regain our market share.

We needed to better understand our value and how we were similar yet uniquely different from our competitors. Knowing where we might be undersold was important so we could explain where we were alike and different from other venues. We needed to highlight to our customers that our value was in the unique offerings we provided, along with the level of service we guaranteed and the overall ambiance that was uniquely us versus Venue B.

As a business owner, I know there are certain parameters I cannot fall below in terms of quality and service for sure and with regard to our profit margins as well. Walmart is boycotted in many small towns, as they can sadly undersell any "mom-and-pop" business working hard at making a living. People like convenience. People like low cost.

People also appreciate and value when service providers go further by assisting their clients with their purchases or when a team member remembers their name, their children's names, the last purchase they made, and how it worked for them. This level of service has value.

In our fast-paced, fast-food, "get it now and get it cheap" mentality, we need to know what people want, and we need to offer more and be better! It's impossible to be all things to all people. As business owners, we need to clearly determine what we want our market sector to be and how to secure a reputation and spot there.

Consider why people purchase higher end brands or go to the Ritz Carlton over the Hampton Inn. Cost is a factor at times, but at other times it's not. You have to know your customers and, if you reduce your margin, by how much and to what purpose. There are times during the year in my business when I am happy to have ten lower margin weddings at my venue rather than no weddings at all.

The numbers have to work and it's your job to know how much it costs to run your business, whether you have customers in your building or your customers are ordering online. This is a key consideration, whether you are a "bricks-and-mortar" establishment or an online service. You need to know how much revenue will keep your team employed and bills paid.

Key, too, in knowing your competition is to study who they are online, in social media platforms, and what people are saying about them. You need to stay on top of the reviews you get (we do weekly audits to assure all communications are positive and if not, to assure that we manage any negative reviews quickly and respectfully). We then go about improving any weak or inconsistent areas within our business. We're only as good as our last review, so staying current on sites where you are listed and reviewed is key.

> **Intend who and what you are and move in the direction of your dreams!**

Claim What You Want to Be

When touring in my one-woman play, I learned that while perception may not be everything, it certainly counts for a lot. If you put yourself out as, "The One and Only" or "Preferred Baker of the Southeast," who can say you are not? You certainly prefer you, certain clients prefer you, hence you are the "Preferred Baker of the Southeast"! Build the field and the people will come, right? Intend who and what you are and move in the direction of your dreams! Again, move forward "as if"—as if you will be successful, as if you will get the lion's share of the work. And then go to work making it so!

Another key differentiator for a business is being considered, an expert or *the* expert or the go-to professional in your field. Offer educational workshops to your clients and blogs that, if not written by you, are penned by others in the field. Create ways for people to recognize what makes your company different, letting them know the heart and soul of what makes your organization tick.

Give them what they want and need. Tap into that desire by being their solution and find out where the competition is or is not doing the same.

Over the years I have worked to make our business as much of a "one-stop-shop" for my clientele as possible. In listening to brides I learned how busy they are—working, often going to school. We position ourselves as the experts in the field (we are), by not just adding services and products they need, but by aligning with partners who can join us in providing what our clients need.

It's not just one service or product that will make clients like you ahead of the competition, but the combination of what you provide, how you provide it, and the timeliness of your communication. How people feel they are treated by you and your team, and the overall bond you work to create to gain their trust and ultimately their respect and their business, make a demonstrable difference to someone seeking a service.

I am not in our main office every day but often working offsite at another office or am traveling. My name is associated with my company's brand and is a big part of my company whether I am there or not. Carl House can stand on its own, as I designed it that way. I am branding both my company and me as a professional as I work in other areas as a consultant, speaker, and writer.

You need to make a choice of how much you want and need to be working in your business every day and how important your personal name is to the brand or not. When living, Colonel Sanders certainly didn't need to be at each store to sell chicken!

How you position your company in your industry, the awards you are nominated for and win, your giving to the community makes a difference. Your team's availability to work on industry association committees to make an impression and contribute to the good of your industry matters. Touch-ins with current and former clients all make a lasting impression that your competition may or may not be doing.

Go ahead, be brave, be the best! With some creativity and a little eye-spy, secret agent work, you can create an organization that exceeds even your expectations!

CHAPTER 10
Cash Is and Always Will Be King! Have a Reserve!

Number one, cash is king . . . number two, communicate . . . number three, buy or bury the competition.
—Jack Welch
American Business Executive, Author, and Chemical Engineer

"If broke people are making fun of your financial plan, you're on track.
—Dave Ramsey
American Financial Author, Radio Host, Television Personality, Speaker

Cash Is King! Have A Reserve! Cash Is King! Have A Reserve! Cash Is King! Have A Reserve! Cash Is King! Have A Reserve! Cash Is King! Have A Reserve! Cash Is King! Have A Reserve! Cash Is King! Have A Reserve! Cash Is King! Have A Reserve! Cash Is King! Have A Reserve! Cash Is King! Have A Reserve! Cash Is King! Have A Reserve! Cash Is King! Have A Reserve!

You get my point! Businesses need cash to operate. Similarly, you should not work for free. Even if you bankroll the money, consider payment for whatever role you assume. If you want to give the funds away, or allocate them someplace within the company, fine, but place a monetary value on your contribution to the company.

Understanding the "Money Part" of Your Business

During the start-up phase, you might need to wait for your first paycheck while you live on savings, a mate's paycheck, or the dowry Aunt Betsy left you. Figure in your break-even point, what it costs to run your business, how soon you can hire help so you don't burn out, and what you will pay yourself within a projected "when"!

Without a plan, your best intentions might succumb to circumstance, and that's no way to run a company. Just as you put together a plan for starting your company (you did, didn't you?), you need a financial plan to keep it running. One of my first "hires" was a bookkeeper, as this is not my area of expertise or passion. It was key for me to have an experienced person set up my books, account for monies in and monies out and, together, to create a budget. Our budget considered proposed spending, including marketing, salaries, association fees, and my bricks and mortar costs, which included the cost of the large loan to remodel my building.

Have an idea of your level of risk aversion. Not everyone is comfortable with large debt, regardless the potential return on the loan with a healthy business. When I started my business, my business partner and I didn't have a clear plan;

our debt began accumulating. The amount I needed to bring in each month became larger and larger as did my stress on how much business I needed to secure monthly. This amount was necessary to service my loan and pay other growing monthly expenses, including payroll.

I soon learned to become more comfortable with my capabilities in servicing my loans and expenses. I suggest you be more intentional about where you want your financial responsibilities to fall. Even with a great level of care, surprises are as inevitable as sunburn on the beach!

Financial guru Dave Ramsey is on a crusade to help people get out of debt. Though I look forward to a day when my debt is lowered, or gone, had I not borrowed money to begin my business, I would not have a business. I needed capital to get going, just as most people in business do. Not all debt is created equal, though a plan to minimize your debt and to live with a frugal mentality, paying off your debt as you go, will give you great peace of mind.

I spoke with a seasoned entrepreneur once who shared that he did not have stress, but rather "gave" stress. I was uncertain what he meant. He shared that there were times when he stressed out others, but that he did not have stress himself. Astonished, measuring my own, "stress-o-meter," I asked how that could be. He said, "I have a large pile of money that takes care of just about everything I need."

Though I remember his comment sounding cocky at the time, I reflected on his statement and realized that a large portion of my stress did come from the constant need for a high level of cash flow. I considered, too, how having a large pile of cash would give a level of peace. I recall my father's admonition: "money may not be everything, but it ranks right up there with oxygen."

—Bob Banta

I agree with Dave Ramsey who says, "Winning at money is 80 percent behavior and 20 percent head knowledge. Most of us know what to do, but we just don't do it."

My business had wonderful cash flow in 2008, but terrible sales. In 2009, as did many others, we suffered in that most of our business is booked a year in advance. Most businesses fail for lack of cash flow more than lack of profit. Our profit margins were fine; we just didn't have enough business coming in to satisfy payroll and other expenses. As business owners we need to educate ourselves in the big picture overview of what is needed financially in our business to first, stay alive and second, to prosper.

Without a good cash flow forecasting model, business owners often fail to anticipate a cash shortage and run out of money, forcing them to cease operations even though they have active customers.

I recall once asking an accounting person I had at the time. "How is our cash flow looking?" I inquired.

"Great," she said, "we have money in the bank!"

As delighted as I was to hear that we had money in the bank, my real concern was how we were looking six months to a year out. Our busy season is during the spring and the fall with weddings. We however need to be bringing in enough money to satisfy the leaner months of January and February, to be discerned through forecasting of projected expenses against cash flow in the future.

Good Debt, Bad Debt

As shared earlier, I needed to borrow a large sum of money to start my company and then more, after some poor decisions and a shift in the economy. There are many decisions I would have made differently to prevent unnecessary leaking of funds from my company. I have a dear friend who is an enormously successful businessperson, a totally behind-the-scenes personality who works hard, humbly, and strategically.

To this day I don't think she's ever bought a piece of clothing at a retail store. She instead frequents yard sales and buys anything she needs at outlets or other places sure to give her what she wants or needs at a far reduced price from what most of us are accustomed. Eating out to her is an unnecessary extravagance. Far from denying herself pleasures (her preference is saving for favored Harley Davidson Motorcycles, of which she owns thirty), she early on adopted a practice of frugalness that has allowed for her wealth and development of a razor sharp business savvy!

Having learned through her own, "school of hard knocks," she tragically assumed debt from a former business partner to whom she'd given the business. She was charged one million dollars in back tax debt after her former business partner let the business fall into decline and filed for bankruptcy. Tragically, my friend hadn't filed the proper papers when giving him her share of the company and her name was never properly removed from the company's legal documents.

My friend dutifully paid those governmental back taxes throughout a nine-year period. These sorts of lessons either make or break us. In her case, it strengthened her resolve and made her a more seasoned, discerning, and successful entrepreneur!

Far from suggesting you deny yourself some of the things you work hard for, consider instead being selective as to where and when you spend your money. In addition, assure you are doing things in your business correctly—exiting a business so you have no more liability!

Before you spend on anything outside the bare necessities, know how much you have outside the "necessary." Scores of financial books assert putting a certain percentage of funds toward wealth-building, through investments and other income multipliers.

Monies should also be allocated for emergency situations, which will arrive, for me, one year to the sum of $28,000 worth of new air conditioning units needed; another year, a five-digit sum for an IT upgrade. One of my most disheartening financial surprises to date was $37,000 in back taxes for not better understanding where certain items we charge for had become subject to tax. If there are monies left *after* allocating to "necessities," savings, and a needed emergency fund, do with it what you will and enjoy!

Necessary Losses

The unfortunate hits we take and unnecessary losses are actually *necessary* losses enabling us to learn. These are lessons that if we're paying attention, make us wiser—hopefully not bitter—aware, and sharp. My friend came up with both the strength and moxie to satisfy the enormous debt she was faced with, despite the consistent bullying and other governmental knocks on her door. She became stronger and wiser.

Cash is king and the smarts to know what you do to build cash flow, manage debt and expenses, while saving for the time you'll need the monies, because you *will* need them, is key. With that, be sure to have the proper paperwork and insurance policies in place to protect yourself from a lawsuit or attack from the government should you not have the proper compliances in place.

The great news is that money is energy and there is always more out there to be earned. Be smart, know what you need, have a great saving plan, excellent forecasting tools, awareness of your market, and marketing plan to bring in the cash. Learn to diversify into new profit centers and, finally, enjoy the things in life you are meant to enjoy as you reap the bounty of your own hard and savvy, smart work!

CHAPTER 11
Snakes, Serpents and Vultures!

Among predatory beasts, any display of weakness is an invitation to attack.
—Dean Koontz
American novelist, *The Odd Thomas* Series 4-Book Bundle

The best revenge is to be unlike him who performed the injury.
—Marcus Aurelius , Philosopher, Roman Emperor

I learned from my mother to be *strong*, hold up against injustice, and to *survive* amidst adversity. I learned from being thrown about in business to *stand up* against injustice and to *flourish* from adversity.

My "Pollyanna" upbringing—looking for the best in all people—hasn't changed. I've learned instead to discern more appropriately. Not everyone has my best interests in mind and some folks are just seasoned predators. I've met my share. They've cost me a bundle, not in hard cold cash alone, but in extraordinary mental anguish.

Being with "What Is"

I was working out at a new fitness studio in Atlanta recently, doing a mixture of Pilates, torture, and stuff to make you howl and sweat. At one point, as I endeavored to hold a plié while on tippy toes, I was crunching in my glutes at the insistence of my instructor, Julie. My entire lower body muscles began to shake with fierce tremors; my eyes clenched shut, teeth in full grit.

Noticing my supreme discomfort Julie shouted, "Yes BB, *yes!* This is where the transformation happens. Hold there, hold there, *hold there!*"

Our instinct is to run away from pain, but staying awhile in the discomfort, experiencing what it is, we can better determine how to manage it differently or avoid it moving forward.

Those of us in the dating field know about predators and how they can smell our vulnerabilities, our need for love and affection, to be wanted, nurtured. They exist in the world of business, too, and I'll admit to being astonished every time I've made a misstep in judgment.

I learned that being a strong person, or personality, has little to do with warding off troubling invaders when you embrace also a willingness to be vulnerable. I found the need to manage both my strength and vulnerability with discernment, as each is important for both business and personal growth.

I found I needed to learn to manage both my strength and vulnerability with discernment, as each is important for both business and personal growth.

If it Feels Wrong, You're Probably Right

Snakes and serpents slither and vultures prey upon the weak and dying. I found that so do some professionals who volley for your business. As seasoned salespeople, they find out what you need, where you struggle, and what builds your areas of low self- esteem or a perceived lack of business savvy. I've allowed this to happen on numerous occasions, one was with a charismatic business coach I hired just after the turn of the economy.

Devastated with challenges within my business, he appealed to my ego mostly, and with a chest full of bravado he offered to be my "champion." I literally felt tears well up in my eyes, thankful that at last someone saw my talent and self-worth and would "Help me, oh please, help me!"

He encouraged areas within me that needed encouraging and also referred a host of, "professionals" to "save" the many areas of my business that were not doing well, or so I thought. He was like the man who came to town offering up his magic stone soup. He brought the stone while others supplied a variety of desired ingredients for the fine and hearty soup.

After working with him I was soon convinced that I didn't have the right skills to properly hire, looking at my then track record when things shifted in the economy. I had to let people go followed by a host of hurried and ill-fitting new-hires. Sadly I soon learned that even his recommended providers of services ("vegetables") for my "business soup" lacked talent or value.

Doubling conveniently as a recruiter, saying, "I want to help you," he suggested I let him recruit two new-hires at a greatly reduced fee. His reduced fee was a financial stretch for me and by the time I got the people hired, my final bill came to $11,000 *higher* than discussed. I was aghast but admittedly, so smitten by his supposed talent and willingness to help, I was sure I must have heard the fee incorrectly.

Another part of me knew exactly what I'd heard. I had no contract, only my integrity and I certainly didn't want to insult him or doubt his word. He insisted that of course this was the fee, I must have heard wrongly.

Predators make us feel special, unique, and as though we deserve the extra attention of their coveted savvy and "know-how." Conversely, they know how to respond to our weaknesses and areas of self-doubt. He played me as smoothly as an Atlantic City card shark!

I later found he had little knowledge of my industry or whom I should be hiring. Each of his recommended new-hires proved a more ridiculously worse fit than the next. One recommended recruit I found entirely ill-fitting and let her go before the trial three-month mark. Soon I was mixed up with Department of Labor allegations and a hearing, as she was insisting on unemployment payment despite her gross lack of qualifications. Sadly, I had no documented infractions and a refund for this recruited misfit was not an option.

Next came the EEOC (Employee Equal Opportunity Commission), accusing me of prejudicial intent. Why I'd pay a recruiting fee in the five digits to bring an individual into my company, to then release that person within three months for prejudicial reasons was quite a stretch.

With attorney fees, settlements, recruiting fees, and her three-month salary, I paid more than $60,000 for the short time she spent in my company at the recruiter-coach's recommendation. I was in shock, totally stunned at how this scenario played out and, caught in governmental systems, I began to respect him less and less.

My coach conveniently disappeared during this time. A showman, I was shocked that a performer such as I am didn't have better radar. We see what we want to see, and at the time I had little confidence to feel I could alone move through the many challenges I was facing within my company, and how they were personally affecting me. Perhaps the sting of my own misjudgment was too much to bear. I couldn't piece together how someone could be so criminal, unaccountable, and disrespectful to *me*! It took me another eight months to realize my poor choice in selecting a "champion" for my business development.

Embracing the Lesson

I criticize my own need for approval, self-doubt, lack of awareness, and gullibility for what occurred. I was far from powerless. More than suffering disappointment or abuse, I learned instead how powerful I was, what good hiring judgment I could develop, and business savvy I had as I dug deep. It wasn't the coach who got me through the shift in the economy, but my own moxie, despite the financial and emotional challenges he added to my burden at the time.

Though this wasn't my last incident of naiveté and misjudgment, my huge takeaway is that I had gained a greater measure of discretion that only experience can teach. Coaching can be extremely beneficial and can catapult your business forward, if your coaching ally is mindfully chosen.

> Though this wasn't my last incident of naiveté and misjudgment, my huge takeaway is that I had gained a greater measure of discretion that only experience can teach.

I remember returning from the EEOC mediation feeling dirty, exhausted, alone and, while not defeated, certainly beat up. I came home to find that one of my cats very uncharacteristically had pooped in my bedroom. I came home to "shit." It seemed fitting.

I went for a walk with my dogs in a nearby field to clear my head. I remember my dogs finding fresh horse poop and rolling in it, gleefully, not something *they* characteristically did.

It dawned on me, when things feel like shit, roll in it, embrace it, smell it, taste it, and then let it go. *Let it go.* And, after that day, I did. Having experienced the full stench and unpleasantness of it all, I could now let it go. I could let the "shit" fertilize my "garden"—my business. And, given time, it did!

It dawned on me, when things feel like shit, roll in it, embrace it, smell it, taste it, and then let it go. Let it go.

Putting a Protective Process in Place

Move slowly and get references for both employees and professionals you're looking to hire to assist you in managing and growing your business. Keep the personal out of these relationships, or it will be a disservice to both parties, especially to you. In any role, you find good and bad fits. There are certainly right-fitting employees and business coaches with which to work. Choose carefully!

Get everything in writing and, certainly with employees, document, document, and document again, everything that happens. Help people to be successful and when their behaviors or performance is not what is expected, share that with them. Guide them into expected behaviors through careful documentation and training. Have a witness in the room as you give notes to assure that what was said can be backed up with another set of trusted ears.

Clearly stated job descriptions and requirements of the job prevent guesswork in any position, as does a clear company manual and worksite specific manual, to outline how you work within your company. Include clearly outlined human resource (HR) guidelines as well. These documents are meant to protect both you and your employees with determined rules of conduct. Clear vision, mission, and culture statements will help guide behaviors within your company and keep undesired behaviors in check. An employment contract is advisable to clearly define expectations and to protect both parties.

As for the predators, they'll continue to exist. It takes all manner of personalities and worldviews to fill out our population of humans on the planet. Don't spend time in the past where poor judgments were made, but trust your instinct and heightened discretion, move forward with clear intentions, and remember that if something feels wrong, you're probably right!

CHAPTER 12
Adversity Rocks: Leveraging Your Mistakes
and Steering Your "Ship" Toward Success!

So you think that you're a failure, do you? Well, you probably are. What's wrong with that? In the first place, if you've any sense at all you must have learned by now that we pay just as dearly for our triumphs as we do for our defeats. Go ahead and fail. But fail with wit, fail with grace, fail with style. A mediocre failure is as insufferable as a mediocre success. Embrace failure! Seek it out. Learn to love it. That may be the only way any of us will ever be free.

—Tom Robbins
American Novelist
Even Cowgirls Get the Blues

Sure applause feels better than a booing crowd. Great reviews build our self-esteem and happy, smiling clients let us know we're doing things right. It's the poor reviews that teach us the most. Adversity is a necessary proponent of all growth.

A worthy goal will require stamina, persistence, tenacity, and grace—grace with regard to your own "unknowing." If everyone were able to start and maintain a business, there'd be more successful business owners. As the Roman teacher and Philosopher Epictetus said somewhere between 55 and 75 AD:

Tentative efforts lead to tentative outcomes. Therefore, give yourself fully to your endeavors. Decide to construct your character through excellent actions and determine to pay the price for a worthy goal. The trials you encounter will introduce you to your strengths. Remain steadfast . . . and one day you will build something that endures; something worthy of your potential.

Creating Solutions

Years ago I lived awhile in Columbus, Ohio, where I was studying dance. A year earlier I had shared with a favored theatre mentor that I felt I was rather clumsy and wished I could move better.

He suggested, "Take time to learn to dance."

"But my career!" I countered. "I want to get moving with my performing career."

Patiently he smiled, "Learn to dance. It'll help your career and you'll have greater confidence. Your career will wait. Build your foundation."

He was right. He was nearly always right. He had more than fifty years of experience more than my own.

So off I went to The Ohio State University, which had a respected dance program and I learned to "move better." The training did help my confidence as a performer and person. I felt more at ease and confident within my body. I later realized this was an important step in developing "my career"!

I waitressed at the time to pay my bills and was a novice runner. I hurt my knee running and was unable to work a long shift. I needed to take a few weeks off to allow my knee to sufficiently mend.

To bring in additional monies while studying dance, I contracted to do occasional radio and television work, mostly commercials. I also developed a children's show where I told stories for birthday parties. While working and studying in Maine, years before, I had learned to do simple acrobatic type moves and to juggle as I worked with some terrific street performers, jesters, clowns, dancers, and acrobats. I added juggling and walking on my hands to my repertoire, while performing for the amusement of the children at their parties.

During the time when I was injured and in need of money, I knew that the 4th of July was coming and that many people would be gathering to see fireworks.

The skilled performers I worked with brought in piles of cash with their street work in popular places like Faneuil Hall in Boston and other tourist destinations. I considered doing a bit of juggling and my top-hat tricks and then pass the hat as I'd seen my friends do to bring in some dollars while folks waited for the fireworks.

I didn't need to walk on my bad knee much, just stand awhile juggling, first balls, then clubs. Though I'd not done it a lot, I thought I'd toss my always-exciting fire sticks, as well. A simple three-throw cascade was something I had confidence performing in the past, and fire was a surefire crowd pleaser!

Off I went in my black and white performing outfit, ready with my hat and zippered bag for anticipated money. I parked my car on the outskirts of the park where the fireworks would be displayed. A few people began gathering as I took a deep breath and started my simple ball routine. With a little dialogue back and forth with the audience, I then brought out my juggling clubs and soon after, fire sticks.

Immediately people began to applaud, bringing dollars and more dollars in, filling my top hat! I was elated and encouraged!

"Hey," I thought, "maybe I can give up waitressing."

I knew I was entirely out of the league of my street performing friends. My real interest and talent was writing monologues and creating character sketches, but this was a nice switch and I certainly needed the money.

More people began gathering in every direction as the sun began to set. I'd dropped a fire stick but quickly gathered it up and continued on. As dusk moved steadily in, I realized I'd never rehearsed fire sticks without being able to see the handles. I could feel my grip tighten. With the fire being bright, handles black, and darkness moving in, I began dropping one and then another of the bright fire sticks.

When two more sticks dropped, the audience grew quiet. From the back of the crowd, like a distant fog horn:

"Boooooo. Booooooooooo."

I froze. I forced myself to pick up the fire sticks and another dropped, then one more. Suddenly, like a descending pack of wolves, I heard five, ten, maybe twenty voices sounding with the refrain, "Booooo! *Booooo!*"

I continued with no greater luck and soon fifty loud voices could be heard, saying what no performer, no *person* wants to hear. "Booo! Go *home! Go home!*"

Suddenly, by my side was a towering, muscular man in a green beret. I thought I was being arrested for performing so badly! I soon learned he was there to assure that the crowd remained orderly and to help me leave safely from this den of wolves, eager to eat me alive! I had a pile of money, was hated by the audience, and was limping. He saw my vulnerability and the desperate look on my face.

"Let me help you out of here. What can I carry?"

"Please carry my bag of money. I really need it."

He smiled the smile of an angel.

With Mr. Green Beret by my side, I limped off holding his arm, defeated and worn, but greatly relieved he showed up, hoping only to get to my car and rest my knee. When I got to the parking lot there were scores of people sitting on my car and on the other cars in the lot, blocking the way to get out. The fireworks had just started.

Timidly I asked, "Would you all please move? I need to leave."

A woman sitting on my car protested, *"The fireworks are starting bitch,"* along with other similar epithets.

Nice crowd! I was thankful for the presence of my green-topped guardian who, with a stern eye, moved the grumbling crowd aside. My car parted the people like cattle on the road. I glanced out the window as I left the lot and caught his eye. He gave me a wink to tell me I was safe.

I went home sodden, exhausted, discouraged, but not defeated. I remember thinking, "If I can survive that humiliation and keep my confidence, I can survive and do anything!"

It was a defining moment! I'll never forget the importance of that lesson and experience, or the angel who showed up right when I needed him.

We *are* safe! We are guided, if we'll listen, and what occurs in our life can be viewed as a gift, or not. I choose gift, and will look for the advantage in any situation. I will also look for its message and gift in any circumstance that might otherwise work to pull me down or apart.

We *are* safe and need to remember that. We are guided, if we'll listen, and what occurs in our life can be viewed as a gift or not.

Envisioning Your Desires

My greatest wish is that I might fully exercise my potential and purpose in this lifetime, that I might prove of good service, and do good works.

Consider the epiphanies gained from adversities you've encountered. Reflect on how your relationships improved as you learned how *not* to treat others. Consider that, in not watching your monies or your health, you possibly suffered from ill health, or doing without, to gratefully learn a new and better way to manage those areas of your life.

And then there are the things that happen in our lives that have little to do with what we did or didn't do, that we prepared or didn't prepare for, the calamities, the unthinkable happenings in our life. Someone dies or is injured recklessly. I've had dear friends who have suffered unthinkable assaults. We turn our head a moment and our child is gone, a rare affliction is brought onto us, what we value most is taken.

I have little idea why certain circumstances come to some and not to others. I'm unsure why bad people aren't brought to justice and why good people are wrongly penalized. I do know that life seems random, though perhaps is not. I know, too, that though I assert and crave a measure of control in my life, there is so much that is not in my power except how I manage what comes.

When adversity strikes, my best friend and I give one another one full day to vetch, complain, act the victim, cuss, and carry on. It is then time to move forward, let go of what hurts as best we can, and begin to heal and create better solutions.

We've all met people who hang on dearly to their hurts, who refuse to move on to new ground but again and again bring up why they were wronged and how they intend revenge.

> *An eye for an eye will only make the whole world blind.*
> —Mahatma Gandhi

I suggest you choose your thoughts and words wisely, as they hold great power. I can either hope my business will be successful or I can intend all good and create a plan for moving forward "as if" I will be successful. There are a multitude of books out that assist in preparing us for an intentional life, helping us to become aware of what Henry Ford put quite plainly: "Whether you think you can, or you think you can't—you're right."

With the blur of technology, media, and other people's thoughts, beliefs, and ideas in your head, consider what you *know* to be true. If you don't know it yet, but desire it, hold that thought and belief firmly in your mind and in your heart and begin to watch things change.

Neal Donald Walsh wrote a book called, *Conversations with God.* In it he asserts that as soon as you claim what you desire as being present in your life—"I am prosperous"—expect everything that is *not* that to show up in your world to test your faith. Your car breaks down, you lose your job, you thought your insurance was paid up but wasn't when you needed it. We must act prosperously, even when things are not going our way. We must carry ourselves with the same confidence as when abundance is easily seen.

> We must act prosperously, even when things are not going our way. We must carry ourselves with the same confidence as when abundance is easily seen.

Consider the challenge for people growing up in poverty or in abusive situations. I work with a wonderful organization called The Jeannette Rankin Foundation. Jeannette Rankin was a proponent of women's rights and was the first woman to be elected to the United States Congress in 1916. Upon her death, Rankin left a portion of her Georgia estate to assist "mature, unemployed, women workers." Ever since the Foundation was chartered in 1976, with $16,000 seed money from Rankin's estate, it has been helping mature, low-income women succeed through education.

These women are single mothers, typically living in poverty situations with little to no education. They are possibly involved with drugs or in domestic violence situations. The Foundation has awarded seed money for an education for these women. Since 1976, the Foundation has raised more than $2 million to help more than seven hundred women move into productive, fulfilled lives. It's from this small bit of support, emotionally and financially, that these women have lifted themselves out of adverse situations. By seeing the alternatives available and doing the necessary work, these women now successfully move in new and better directions.

If you don't have a support network to move in the direction of your dreams, find one. Whether through business associations, a like-minded CEO roundtable group, reputable coaching, respected peers, family, or friends, find support. None of us succeeds in a vacuum.

Consider what publications or books might inspire new thinking and what workshops might keep you uplifted and moving in the direction you wish. What thought or intention fills your mind as you wake in the morning, and what negative mind-sets are you working to release? Initiate the changes you want to see in your life.

Assess Your Current Thinking

For ages after the challenges I encountered in 2008 through 2011 in particular, with certainly a share of smaller ones in any given month since then, I realized that daily I was poised for bad news. I would wait for a call to tell me the air conditioning was out, just before an event involving 250 people coming to my venue, or the chef was sick and we had no back up—any number of adverse scenarios.

Though I'd succeed among the worst of scenarios, learning preventative measures to avoid calamities and a growing confidence that I could manage challenges that would come, I was still poised for disaster. Challenge will come, as that is life and we get through them. I found that stressing at the advent of an imaginary calamity is wasted energy focused in the wrong direction.

I realized I needed to have my eye and mind on positive things instead. I began looking to create and to reflect on the many positive things happening within my business. My extremely happy customers far outweighed any client or guest who shared discontent with us. I made a list of all the challenging situations I'd encountered, lived through, and learned from since opening my business.

Equally, I listed the enormous list of good things that happened, jobs created, wonderful employees, smart new profit centers, opportunities, and revenue growth. I listed the things I was looking to develop—my book, my talks, plans for a second venue in the works, a new television series, and the abundant good fortune that was currently in my life.

Intend the Good You Wish to Experience

Make a list, embrace all you've learned and the solutions you've created to manage challenges moving forward. List the people who are there to assist and support you. Create another list of other new people you'd like to bring into your life, whether you've met them yet or not. Intend the good you want to attract into your life, and see about enjoying each day and the blessings brought to you, both in joyful experiences and the ones that create your own growth and moxie. Share your wealth, mostly in wisdom, with kindness and with good intent.

We can focus on the pain or the challenge of adversity, or we can wake each day with gratitude for all that we are presented with in life. Know that you have only a measure of control of what happens in your life. Do your best to roll with the current. Know, too, that only you can bring the peace you desire to any given moment. Breathe, as a new moment is just ahead of you!

CHAPTER 13
Paying It Forward, Again and Again and Again

We rise by lifting others.

      —Robert Ingersoll, Orator, Attorney, Politician

Be the change you want to see in the world.
      —Mahatma Gandhi, Preeminent Leader of Indian Nationalism

Life is made up of moments. The present moment is all that really exists and with each moment we have a choice.

I, too, am often living forward and find myself way ahead of the moment and, frankly, miss my life. Like a racehorse, I'm built that way. Even so, as I reflect on the passage of time, the things worth fretting about are minimal if I have a support system, the ability to learn and adapt, and a belief in something bigger than my human experience. I consider our world one of abundance and choice. I find the need to regularly encourage myself to slow a bit and return to now, where all the action *really* is!

It is through mindfulness that we return to where we are and where we can do the most good. Noticing what is needed within ourselves or for others within each moment is where we ultimately thrive. It is in those moments I find the greatest peace. The key is to return to the moment, again and again and again.

> Noticing what is needed within ourselves or for others within each moment is where we ultimately thrive.

Managing Your Stressors

The stressors of cash flow, the challenges of managing people, and the concerns of staying compliant with quickly shifting governmental regulations, are challenging for sure. With the need to be nimble in an ever-changing economy, owning a business can make you feel that you're raising and supporting a very large family with vastly different needs and personalities. The stressors are not to be minimized.

I was informed last year that a dear friend was diagnosed with multiple sclerosis (MS). Multiple sclerosis is a potentially debilitating disease in which the body's immune system eats away at the protective sheath (myelin) that covers the body's nerves. My friend has lost her ability to walk and to speak, though is mentally very aware. Her long-term prognosis is not encouraging.

It's easy to measure our woes and challenges on our own "Richter scale" while wearing blinders to the rest of the world. This is easy to do when our stressors are great and we feel the responsibility of delivering to clients, cash flow to keep jobs, and seeking our own personal contentment. We all have individual burdens to carry. Some burdens prove fatal, others stressful and annoying, while others, perhaps taxing to some, are easy for us to weather.

Gaining Perspective

When I was young, a babysitter of mine shared that she had, a year before, broken up with her boyfriend of many years. She was inconsolable. She had never experienced that kind of loss, fear of being unattached, and sense of defeat. She shared her grief with her grandmother, who admonished her by saying, "Get over it. I lost a husband in the war; losing a boyfriend at your age is nothing!" Breaking up with her boyfriend was far from nothing to this young woman. It was the most devastating loss she had experienced in her life at that point.

In a country and culture consumed by technology—texting, tweeting, Facebook and more—it's easy to forget that there is a living, breathing human being on the other end of our communication. There is a person who has, or had, a mother and father who loved them, who spent time as a baby and a vulnerable child, and who can be very hurt by words, by actions, and by inconsiderate acts.

Some of the comments I hear people making online, without being face-to-face with another, shock and disappoint me. I wonder at the thoughtless and hurtful nature of such lashing out and am disquieted witnessing such anger and disrespect.

We periodically offer events for the public at my venue and this year we held our popular Mother's Day Brunch. We post our menu in advance and market the event at least six weeks ahead of the date. We offer a wide variety of breakfast options, brunch items, a plethora of assorted desserts, salads, and several meat options as well. We have a price for children and another for adults with children five and under coming at no cost. We offer a variety of juices, milk for the kids, our famous southern peach iced tea, and scrumptious Carl House signature coffee.

I attended this year's event and made sure to visit all the tables, making sure our guests were happy while assisting my team in delivering "over-the-top" service. Carl House is not a restaurant and Mother's Day brunch is a different type of event than our more typical weddings or other private events. We work to represent our brand, as the event serves more as a marketing opportunity for us than a, for-profit event. We often do not break even at this event, but create exposure to people who may not have visited Carl House before.

The event was a lot of work for everyone, from the marketing crew and weekday workers to the people who worked the actual event. We need our entire team to make this Mother's Day event happen. Our floral designer assured we had beautiful "tablescapes," our chef worked three events before the Sunday event with only four hours of sleep, as most items are made fresh. Only a few items can be prepped beforehand. It was a gargantuan effort and worth every bit of work it took to create the event for the community and for the opportunity to show off what we can do!

At the end of the event, once everyone had left, we were delighted with all the comments we received from guests. One woman asked to see the chef as she was elated with the food and service provided. At the end of each event my team has a, "post mortem" of sorts, discussing what went well and where we can improve. We left tired but knowing we had created a win and that all the guests seemed very happy. It was a great event despite a few, "behind the scenes" challenges that are, from time to time, part of any production, hidden from view and managed.

After my fourteen-hour shift (longer for much of my team), I came home to answer a few e-mails and found a lengthy e-mail forwarded from our marketing assistant who asked me how to handle it. The e-mail was from a woman who attended our brunch with her family, friends, and several children. She spared no words in venting her discontent.

In a long paragraph with no breaks, she shared how she felt we were not children friendly because we had no chicken fingers or "mac-and-cheese" or soda. She said that our desserts ran out. They didn't—we merely had a broad assortment and not every variety was available throughout the entire two seatings.

She compared us to several other places she'd attended that hosted Mother's Day events. She felt two protein options was not enough (we actually offered three), and said there was a mix-up with the mimosas that, though it was sorted out, was upsetting to her. She thought the pork tenderloin was overly salty. She noted also that her mother-in-law ate so little that she didn't think it was worth the price for what she actually ate. She added that she thought the pricing for kids' meals was too high because her children found few items that pleased them.

Overcome with exhaustion, I had to catch my breath. I shared with my marketing assistant that I would manage the situation. I thought long and hard before responding. I value all feedback, though was taken aback at both the accusatory tone of her message and surprised remembering the guests at her table. Despite a mix-up with a mimosa ordered, they seemed content.

I wrote directly that I was very disappointed to hear that her experience at my venue did not meet her expectations. I shared that in going into business and with the long hours and risks a business owner takes, the last thing I ever want is to displease a customer. I shared that her feedback was of great value and that I agreed the pork was a bit on the salty side. I told her that I would certainly consider more children-friendly options in the future and was sorry her children didn't like any of our numerous desserts and that her mother-in-law found little to enjoy. I also shared that I was sorry for the mix-up with the mimosa and happy that we sorted it out for her guests.

I did share that we had posted the menu online for everyone to see ahead of time. I expressed regret that she was not happy with her experience and offered to return her money for five children's meals and one for her mother-in-law. I thought to myself how sad it was that her mother-in-law could not find anything she liked with more than twenty options of lunch and brunch, including numerous dessert items.

The woman wrote back to me directly, sharing that she didn't expect to hear from the owner and certainly not so quickly. She appreciated my thoughts and concern and was not asking for money returned, though she happily accepted it. She noted that she would tell everyone about us and that this event was a gift from her husband and that she had viewed our menu beforehand.

When You're Uncertain, Express Gratitude

I'm sure there are many different reactions to how I handled this situation. No, the customer is not always right and we cannot please everyone. I considered how her husband must have felt having gifted her with a lovely meal and experience, only to hear bitter complaints and discontent. My team was initially devastated given all the hard work they had done preparing the meal. Other guests had seemed very happy and had told us so without being asked. I told them that we consider all comments seriously so that we might better our offerings and service. We should also consider the source of comments and realize that not everyone will be happy.

My hope was that this woman might consider the source as well and if she did not appreciate our efforts, at least appreciate the gift intended from her husband. I added a piece of my BB Brand Jewelry—a sea pearl with a heart— into the envelope with her reimbursement. It was well worth the money and maybe she'll respond more kindly next time before lashing out. She might instead be a chronic complainer who gets her money refunded at numerous places she visits. It's hard to know, but giving grace is never a bad thing, or considering the source, good or bad.

Be the Change You Want to See

Consider what it takes to change a stressful day for someone—listening, doing some small act of giving, a smile, a cup of coffee, staying late at the office to help another with an assignment. We get cast in roles as employees, owners, and clients. I urge my team to greet everyone who comes through our doors with a smile, offer them a beverage, look them in the eyes, and ask how their day is going, and listen. I encourage this behavior not just for our clients, but within our team as well.

I am overwhelmed with gratitude when a team member asks me if I'd like coffee or food that I provide for us all from the weekend events. With back-to-back meetings on some days, it's enormously thoughtful and I am reminded about the importance of doing the same for others.

Become the Gift-Giver

There are many ways to give and in that act of giving we create fuel for our own living. Consider how as a team you might come together, not just at holiday time, but quarterly to invest time in a cause. Allow others to initiate and take ownership. Let your clients know what is important to you and allow them to join in if they choose.

Lightening the load for others and enabling them to learn and grow is a gift we can all give. I challenge you to weekly assess where your thoughts and actions have taken you that week. Where did you make a positive difference in someone's life through a loving comment, an action, or by sending a kind note?

> **Lightening the load for others and enabling them to learn and grow is a gift we can all give.**

I had a dog named Bert a few years back. I cared for him from the time he was born and held him in my arms as he passed away thirteen years later. I called him my "gift-giver." I'd walk into a room and he'd move quickly to his bone and stuffed animal basket to bring me something—a sock or anything to show his love. I might leave the room for five minutes and return, and again he'd retrieve something, drop it at my feet, and smile his beautiful Bert dog smile.

When I was stressed he knew it and would come close to me and lean on me, reducing my stress with his affection. He was a beautiful creature and taught me so much about being truly loving and sweet. I miss him and the joy and love he extended to me every day.

I traveled through some especially challenging years in my business consumed with fear and living in a state of constant "fight or flight." I remember not long ago stopping a moment as I walked into the cathedral-ceilinged living room in my A-frame style home, the sun shining in through tall, shimmering windows. My animals lay around me fed and happy. I was safe and nurtured in this beautiful space. I could feel myself living in a life forecast with doom, the "shoe" having fallen, the worst having happened. I realized in that moment this was a projection and pure fiction.

From that moment on, my practice each morning was to move from my bedroom into this space and extend thanks and gratitude for the privilege and gift of living in such a beautiful home. I would intend the good I desired and consider what I wished, "done," and so it is! We are more powerful than we often allow.

We have become at times a culture of victims, lawsuit happy, unconscious as to our own ability to find happiness with, "what is." I gingerly handle clients we cannot make happy and grow saddened that despite our very best efforts, some people will never find satisfaction, but instead find all the reasons something is wrong. I do respect every person who comes through my doors. We all deserve to be heard, but we don't all necessarily agree.

Emulate the people who inspire you, who make you feel loved and appreciated. Do so in your own fashion and watch the world change around you. Walking in another's shoes is something many people do better than I, though I am inspired to remember the importance of doing to others as I would have them do for me, or better.

My office in Atlanta is small and sunny and perfect for my needs in the city. It is backed up to an alleyway that is frequented by many of the homeless folks who stay at a shelter not far from my office. I walk my dog, Buddy, down the alley and am greeted with bright smiles. We exchange names and morning greetings. I am reminded of my many blessings and feel thankful for the comforts I enjoy—the ability to work, travel, grow a business, and my dear friends and colleagues.

One woman, Liz, is always quick to tell me she likes my dress or the color of my hair. She asks me for nothing, just gives kind thoughts freely every time I walk down the alley. She feels like an angel and keen reminder to me. I am humbled and consider how I might act as an angel to others, especially to the people who are more difficult to love.

We all need love. We can all benefit from kindness and can give our own circumstances room to grow, improve, and flourish. Perhaps it's a mind-set, I'm not sure. I feel best when I am contributing positively somehow to a situation, and I'll bet you will too!

EPILOGUE

While touring my play years ago, I met a woman in the heart of the bayou, Kay Butler. Ms. Butler wrote a play that took place in Louisiana's Cajun country. I remember one line in particular from her play. She wrote: "All you can do, is all you can do, and all you can do, is enough."

Anyone who makes the move to start a business has a certain amount of drive and ambition. That drive will at times in your business become positively fueled and at other times your tank will sputter on near empty. I know the challenge of needing to rest when demands within the business insist that you continue.

Though I haven't a general panacea on how to help you get through the tough times—the times when exhaustion and dissolution make you wonder why you embarked on such a challenge in the first place. I do know that for me, having a support network of close and dear friends, colleagues, and family has been key. You'll need to find your own balance of self-care, rest, good nutrition, and exercise. Personally, I relish and need the comfort of my home and my animals. Both provide a coveted sanctuary where, if I'll allow myself, I can regroup, rest, and rethink my priorities.

Being driven souls with the desire to exercise our various potentials has its positive and negative aspects. Embrace the parts of you that give you joy and make you feel alive, and similarly the places within yourself that feel like your less than desirable qualities. It's the mixture of each that makes up wonderful you.

Others may not know how to embrace you or celebrate you, but you must, with all your perfect imperfections seek to find the beauty in it all and the joy in every day. Being human has no absolutes. We'd be wise to embrace each of the moments we are afforded as best we can. Consider gratitude as often as you can remember!

Our stay on the planet is, relatively speaking, quite brief. Make your contribution matter if you can. Embrace whatever strengths you have and let those around you shine as they exercise their talents. There is no "perfect" in business any more than there is the "perfect" life, except in our embracing of "what is," learning and growing if we can, and enjoying our unique journey.

As you embrace what you have in your life, your business, and the people in it, make sure that your contributions are of pure intent. Providing jobs, a service or product, an avocation that exercises your talents and interests, are positive. Being profitable is worthy and a bonus for the risks and hard work put forth.

During a most arduous time in my business, I had a clear vision and message from my mother, who had passed away years before. I actually saw her playing cards (which she loved), laughing her distinctive and generous laugh. With a grin the size of a rainbow she looked me directly in the eyes and said:

> Honey, when you're having a tough time, pick yourself up, brush off your knees, dry your tears, take a deep breath, and move forward with love, always with love.
> —Kitty Vogel

Rest in knowing that you are a singular energy and light in this world, worthy of all good. And, celebrate *you* in all that you work to bring to the table in any given day. It's enough! Let the light in where you can or, as Leonard Cohen so aptly wrote in his song "Anthem," released in 1992 on his album, *The Future:*

> Ring the bells that still can ring, forget your perfect offering. There is a crack in everything; that's how the light gets in.

Best wishes and a heart full of respect, admiration, and love to you.

ACKNOWLEDGEMENTS

Special thanks go to so many people. I extend a hearty thank you to every single person who has blessed me with the gifts of their talents, hard work, and dedication to my vision at Carl House.

A thank you, too, goes to the people who didn't work out, who helped create adversities working with me at Carl House. It's those adversities that I most value as they taught me more than any MBA program might promise. It's not through the good reviews where we earn our wisdom and coat of armor, but through the things that pierce our hearts, make us stumble and get up again. I extend a sincere thank you to one and all! We are all only as good as the people we surround ourselves with daily. I am forever grateful.

A very special thank you goes to Robin Ramsey, now my CFO, though a woman who paid it forward to me when I was clearly sinking and then continued to grace me with her many gifts during the shift in the economy and beyond. Your faith and trust in me, along with your loyalty and guidance, "stepping in" and playing a variety of roles when exhaustion nearly struck me down, is a blessing I may never be able to fully repay. You have been my angel and my gratitude is immense. Thank you Robin for all you have done to help Carl House survive and me grow.

Without my soul sister, Lulu White, I'd have crumbled with the weight of it all over the last decade. Your sound behind the scenes business savvy and crystal clear assessment of people and situations continue to mesmerize me. In once relaying something that I shouldn't have shared with another person, I remember going back to you with heartfelt apologies and remorse stating:

"I wasn't thinking. I realize that was something I should have kept between us."

With your characteristic brilliant smile and dark Lebanese eyes, you chirped back:

"BB, my friend, I forgave you before you said it."

Nowhere in life have I experienced the combination of faith, encouragement, trust, wisdom and love extolled by you, dear friend. No amount of gratitude can satisfy the gifts you've so freely given me. An extended thank you in this life and beyond!

Heartfelt gratitude goes to my bevy of beautiful, smart, and resilient women friends. To Liz Reeves, our history and bond over these many years has carried me in more ways than I can express. To talented Karen Montanaro, for your friendship and ability to talk arts and metaphysics with a caring, accepting heart. Your perspective is always an inspiration, as is your commitment to the creative process! To April Wood Reeve, for the love you have extended me over the years, your savvy electronics brain, and the comfort of our wine and cheese talks. Thank you to Sherry "Louise" Wheat, for your forthright honestly, commitment to our friendship, and other-worldly perspectives. I can't think of a fonder friend with whom I'd have fun driving off a cliff! To Janice Darling, for your engaging combination of fun, razor sharp smarts and ability to make me feel smarter, funnier, and more beautiful than I might ever be. And Katja Ridderbusch, for your encouragement to me as a writer, a true gift from such a seasoned writer as yourself. And to Marilee Davis, your support and editing eye have meant a great deal to me. Thank you!

To Tom Webb for your faith in my abilities and creative architectural eye for Carl House; I am grateful for your help and generosity in creating the opportunity for me to see what I might develop, grow, and personally achieve. Heartfelt blessings to you. Thank you to my first and favorite business coach, Lee Huffman, for your support throughout the years and your gracious editing eye. A more dedicated and generous business ally I've yet to meet. Thanks to my benevolent attorney, Michael Dailey, for helping to keep the predators at bay and working to hone my radar with best practices. A warm thank you to my dear friend Bruce Ray; your inspiration for encouraging me to move my body when the pressures of business have kept me too firmly seated, is significant. I appreciate your friendship and that you're so readily available for new adventures!

Thank you as well to my current team at Carl House; thank you for working to keep your eye on the ball at Carl House in new ways, developing processes and accountability protocols to allow me to grow the business. I am thankful for your varied talents and unified commitment to making Carl House shine to the delight of all our valued clients and guests. I am delighted and honored to be working with you all.

ABOUT THE AUTHOR

Boundless energy, impeccable taste, and unrelenting attention to detail are the hallmarks of the singular BB Webb. Her theatrical background has given her an eye for what is creative and original, and it shows in each and every event she produces at her award-winning event venue, Carl House, and with every talk or media piece she delivers.

With a host of awards, in 2014 she was nominated as one of the *Atlantan Magazine's* Women of Power and Influence. In 2012 she was selected as one of 10 Top Female Leaders in North Atlanta and was also honored as Barrow County's "Business Woman of the Year." In 2011, her company, Carl House, was selected as one of the top thirty small businesses in the Southeast and of the top thirty in Atlanta.

In 2009, BB was selected as one of five finalists for the coveted WE Excel Award by the National Association of Women Business Owners, Atlanta Chapter. She appeared as a "Hard Knocks" judge in the CBS program, *The Next Tycoon.* In 2008, *CATALYST Magazine* selected her as one of the top five entrepreneurs to watch in Atlanta and in 2006 she was awarded the "Results Count" recognition by Atlanta Women in Business during the "Crossing Bridges" international businesswomen's conference.

BB writes a successful column for *Southern Distinctions Magazine* and is co-author of a Jim Rohn and Jack Canfield book titled, *Rising to the Top.* She is currently working on a book for young professionals and another for entrepreneurs titled, *Tiny Tips of Wisdom for the Small Business Owner.* She is the creator and former host of the successful cable access television show, *Living Life with Style.*

BB spends time at both her home in Barrow County and her flat in Atlanta along with her dog, Buddy, who she claims, rescued her. She has a head full of ideas for both a future television and stage show, with a focus on business as she knows it, and another highlighting the hilarious revelations of being fifty-plus with a very full bucket list!

To learn more about Carl House visit www.carlhouse.com

To inquire about hiring BB as a speaker or consultant in your business, e-mail info@arrivingwithbbwebb.com

To order books and DVDs or downloads of her talks, and to learn more about BB and her other services, visit www.arrivingwithbbwebb.com

For information on how you can purchase BB's books, contact info@arrivingwithbbwebb.com

For information on signing up to use SendOutCards contact info@carlhouse.com or call 770-586-0095.